Y0-CBX-416

Rewards
and
Business Strategy

People, Pay, and Performance

Howard C. Weizmann and Jane K. Weizmann

CCH INCORPORATED
Chicago

Editorial Staff

Senior Acquisitions Editor	Donald J. Hull
Developmental Editor	Sharon Sofinski
Cover Design	Monika Rimple
Book Design/Production	Phyllis Kaplan
Production Specialist	Kathryn M. Astrom

ISBN 0-8080-0470-0

©2000, CCH INCORPORATED
4025 W. Peterson Ave., Chicago, IL 60646-6085
1 800 248 3248
http://hr.cch.com

To Judy Lukas and Phil Tice,

who taught us about living;

and to our children, Brooke and Haley,

who taught us about life.

Contents

About the Authors

Jane K. Weizmann

Jane K. Weizmann is a senior consultant and the practice leader of Watson Wyatt Worldwide's Washington office Compensation Group. Jane has over twenty years' experience in the compensation field and consults with the firm's clients on all aspects of compensation and performance management programs. She specializes in the strategic design of compensation programs and organizational change. Her recent clients range from large, established employers to small, up-and-coming, high-tech firms.

Prior to joining Watson Wyatt, Jane was manager of compensation for The University of Maryland at Baltimore and for Thomas Jefferson University in Philadelphia. She was also a compensation consultant at Hay Associates. Before that, Jane held significant administrative positions with the U.S. Department of Labor.

Jane is a member of the American Compensation Association, the Society for Human Resource Management, and the Washington Technical Personnel Forum. She holds a master's degree from Eastern Michigan University and a bachelor's degree from Ohio University.

Howard C. Weizmann

Howard Weizmann is the managing consultant of Watson Wyatt's Washington, D.C. office. He is principally responsible for the management of the 300-person consulting office, which provides human resource consulting services to a wide variety of Fortune 50 and other clients. In addition to this role, Howie works with clients in a variety of human resource areas and is a frequent speaker and commentator on current human resource issues.

Before joining Watson Wyatt, Howie was vice president at Aetna Life and Casualty where he directed the health, pension, and communications consulting practices. For four years, he served as executive director of the Association of Private Pension and Welfare Plans (APPWP), a leading employee benefits lobbying group. Prior to that, Howie was the manager of benefits planning and design for Sun Company, Inc., and was a senior attorney in the compensation and benefits area. He helped design and implement one of the first 401 (k) plans in 1982 and one of the first cash balance plans in 1986.

Howie holds a law degree from Georgetown University Law School. He graduated from Ohio University and was a Danforth Graduate Fellow. He received an M.A. from and was a doctoral candidate in anthropology at the University of Michigan.

Preface

Writing a book with another professional requires real partnership. Co-authors need to share a common vision and message. Styles need to mesh and issues must be resolved in ways that leave both parties satisfied. In the end, one hopes that the synergies flowing from the collaboration make the product better than if only one person authored it.

The issues around collaboration multiply when the authors have been married for nearly thirty years. Domestic as well as professional tugs get factored into the equation. Discussing some arcane point while one of us does the dishes, pays bills, or waits for one of our daughters to finish field hockey practice becomes commonplace. We have indeed lived with this book in a way that few others live with a project.

It may seem as surprising to you as it is to us that we wound up writing a book together. We both started out in different places—one of us as an anthropologist and lawyer, the other as a compensation professional and consultant. Common interests and a common employer led to our own professional collaboration on clients and in making joint presentations on the issues discussed in this book. So when we were approached by CCH INCORPORATED to write this book, we saw it as a natural extension of our continuing activities.

We've had fun writing this together. But the real stimulus came less from our personal relationship than from our shared need to tell others what we've learned over the years. A consultant friend told us that his son once asked his wife a question about an issue. When she said, "ask your father," his son responded dolefully by saying, "I don't want to know that much." This is the consultant's curse. By virtue of our work, we are exposed to many different situations and see what has worked and what hasn't. It's the need to share what we've observed and conclusions we've formed that sets those who consult apart from those who have to live with the consequences of our advice. And to some, like our friend's son, even listening to the advice can be overwhelming.

Still, the issues discussed in this book remain compelling to us. Technology and demographics dictated the face of work as much at the end of the twentieth century as it did at the beginning. Building cars, creating uses for electrical power, and building communication networks profoundly affected how people earned their living in the same way the revolution in information technology is reshaping the workplace today. Yesterday's winners were those who harnessed the new technologies to create new products and new ways of producing those products. Today's winners will be no different.

As before, the paradigm for linking a successful strategy to the bottom line relies on a committed, well-directed workforce. What's different is that in the past this was achieved by housing workers together, managing them tightly, controlling information, and providing them with security. Technology, the dearth of workers, and the decline in loyalty to a single company have made the art of linking workers to a strategic vision much harder. How you build commitment to such a vision in today's world is the substance of this book. It's about the *people*, who they are and what they want. It's about *pay* and using it to reinforce alignment. It's also about *performance*, getting the right people to do the right things.

If putting the words on paper was a necessary condition to creating this book, it wasn't, by itself, sufficient to producing it. We are indebted to a wide range of friends and colleagues who helped us get it together. David Friend, Watson Wyatt Worldwide's Eastern region director, and Ira Kay, head of Watson Wyatt Worldwide's Human Capital Practice, sponsored our activity and gave us the time to get it done. Thanks also to Bob Ellis, Watson Wyatt's director of growth and development, and Bob McKee, director of corporate marketing, for supporting this effort and for making resources available that helped transform this proposal from fiction to nonfiction.

We also thank Don Hull from CCH for having the temerity to suggest that we write this book and the patience to stick with us during the ups and downs of the writing process. Thanks as well to our internal editors, Sam Greengard and Charlene Solomon, for pointing us in the right direction and keeping us on course, and to

Sharon Sofinski from CCH for her help and encouragement. And to our friends at Employee Benefit News, Richard Stoltz, et al., who keep inviting us back to speak—thank you for giving us the platform that led to all of this.

Still, nothing would have gotten done without the help of a few key individuals in Watson Wyatt Worldwide's Washington office. Juliet Piekarski, our office director of marketing, who got us the speaking engagement to begin with and helped outline the book. Juliet believed in this project from day one and kept pushing us to get it done. Special thanks as well to our research assistant, Koki Abebe, who provided us with invaluable information and editing, and put all of this together. We greatly appreciate the efforts of Kathy Albritton, who navigated our calendars and made sure we had to enough time set aside to finish the book. Thanks as well to Laura Green and members of the Washington Compensation Practice who made significant contributions over the course of this last nine months. They all endured our "hurry-up-and-wait" style of authorship with irrepressible good cheer, and their confidence in us gave us the confidence to keep going.

Finally, thanks to our colleagues at Watson Wyatt who do the laborious research and survey work that helps folks like us every day in working with clients and in our writing. Nobody does it better!

Jane K. Weizmann
Howard C. Weizmann

Introduction

The real challenge for the year 2000 and beyond is *people*, not technology. Day by day, minute by minute, there is an ever-dawning certainty that human capital is the competitive advantage in today's economy. People are what distinguish our organizations and make them world-class. They give our businesses longevity, and differentiate us from our competitors.

The number one concern for today's organization is: *How do we get to the bottom line? How do we get the results we need?* In other words, *How do we align strategic vision with innovative human resource management to produce superior results?*

Human resource professionals are at the dawn of an entirely new era. Clearly, if human capital is the distinguishing characteristic of successful organizations, HR professionals must transform themselves from personnel managers to workforce architects. It's no longer sufficient to play the role of administrator or to merely define benefits and contributions. We must thoroughly understand our company's vision and ask the right questions. For example, how does our role impact the performance of our organization? How do we devise ways to structure and manage the workforce to accomplish our goals? How do we deliberately use rewards, benefits, and recognition to get the desired results? Who to hire? Who to fire? Who to wire into the processes? And, equally important, who to retire?

This is the new starting point for human resource professionals—one that reflects extraordinary changes in the workplace due to technology and changing attitudes. One that factors in the growing expectations of consumers, shareholders, and employees, who are increasingly altering the way businesses act, and interact. It is a new world, unlike the one we've known.

Adjusting to this new reality is no simple matter. The latter decades of the twentieth century have witnessed a remarkable restructuring of American industry. As competition grew, threatening the very life of organizations, businesses reorganized, squeezing out the layers of fat that made them sluggish and non-competitive. Eventually, prices leveled. Then, periodic waves of consolidation rippled through various industries. That left fewer and fewer competitors standing, and forced old giants in every sector—energy, utilities, health care, telecommunications, automobiles, and beyond—to morph into new entities or find themselves facing extinction.

This new level of competition hasn't come about by chance. Shareholders have served as the driving force behind much of this downsizing and consolidation. Over the last quarter century, they have demanded ever-greater performance and profits. Consequently, the mantra of the era has become *How can we as a company increase shareholder value?* This singular focus represents a fundamental shift in values. Today, the shareholder is king, and the interests of workers have been shoved far down on the list of corporate priorities.

The debris is everywhere. In the 1980s and early 1990s, we witnessed a barrage of newspaper reports and TV news accounts of layoffs. Upheaval in corporate America translated into upheaval in the workplace, as previously faceless statistics took on a new sense of urgency. Suddenly, living, breathing human beings—our friends and neighbors—were without jobs. No one was immune. No one felt safe, as anxiety rippled through all levels of the organization. People who had followed all the rules and dutifully performed their work became victims, and were left feeling bruised and battered. Survivors were left without direction about their jobs and the state of their employer. The sense of security that existed in the "job-for-life" era was suddenly yanked away. Cynical about management's intentions, employees began to question their own promise of loyalty to the corporation. Soon, workplace analysts were talking about the "new employment contract."

This new contract reflected an entirely different mindset, one that dispensed with the deep sense of trust that had long existed in the organization. Suddenly, the contract translated into "take care of yourself." Not surprisingly, senior managers began to bemoan the lack of loyalty and trust. However, no one could predict just how disabling this loss of loyalty would become. It was also impossible to foresee how it would undermine business goals.

Enter the tight labor market of the mid-1990s. The strong, continuous economic upturn put a premium on workers who had talent, knowledge, and skills. It didn't take long for pundits to recognize that shareholder value was directly connected to employee productivity, motivation, and energy. Not surprisingly, employees began to feel free to job hop. In fact, human capital was becoming scarcer than financial capital. Knowledge workers had begun to recognize that advancing individual interests, and not necessarily corporate interests, creates a sense of security.

It is now widely acknowledged that attracting and retaining talented, skilled employees—and motivating them to perform in the best interests of the organization—defines success and failure. As competition challenges organizations to become more customer/client-focused, the key differentiator in the marketplace is not just what product a company sells, but how it sells it. In other words, only talented, energetic, and motivated employees can create outstanding service. Only they can attain the standards of quality that prompt customers to choose a particular company's products and services.

It now falls to creative human resource professionals to harness the successful tools of the past—as well as new ones—to transform demoralized, uncertain organizations into world-class companies with a laser-like customer focus. Companies that attract and retain the best and the brightest will endure, while those that conduct business as usual will likely wither. Research demonstrates that shareholder value is closely tied to workforce commitment and strategic business objectives. Organizations that harness the creativity and energy of their workforce will provide the products and services for new markets. They will form the backbone of this burgeoning global economy.

These forces are pushing human resource professionals to the front lines of enterprise management strategies. They are redefining the role of managers to one that extends beyond the mere design of ad hoc programs or shortsighted solutions. Our goal in writing this book is to help provide a path to success.

As senior consultants at Watson Wyatt, we have personally witnessed this change in mindset and work environment. We have seen firsthand how human resource management practices profoundly influence the success, or failure, of an organization. We've learned that it is not enough to sit idly by; it is crucial to use the right techniques to align an organization's rewards and goals.

We begin by looking at the factors that have created today's workplace and workforce. Chapter One presents a demographic and sociological framework for this new era. Chapters Two and Three illustrate the significant financial implications of tying together a focused human resource strategy with business goals.

Chapters Four and Five probe the realities of the new worker, the new manager, and the new company. Chapter Six takes a traditional—and non-traditional—look at the various incentives required for building organizational success. Chapter Seven explores the notion of modifying the current employee-employer contract, and Chapter Eight offers methods that can transform an organization's work environment.

If people are the business, then the business at hand is about achieving the right reward for all.

chapter **one**

The Forces Shaping the Face of Work

After completing this chapter, you should be able to:

- ◆ Understand the forces that shape the workplace.
- ◆ Identify the demographics of the new workplace.
- ◆ Understand the impact of technology and globalization on today's work environment.
- ◆ Recognize that diversity is a critical business issue in today's marketplace.

Alienation. Perhaps no other word succinctly characterizes the relationship between management and labor during the twentieth century.

Textbooks, scholars, consultants, and the media have long painted a picture of workers who feel deeply estranged from management because they do not own the means of production or because they have no stake in the product or services they provide. Some go so far as to argue that worker alienation is the inevitable outcome of the employer-employee relationship in a capitalist economy. They point to the profusion of strikes, disputes, sick-ins, sabotage, and general apathy that at times seems to envelop organizations in almost every industry.

Unfortunately, this argument overlooks the basic fact that numerous organizations have succeeded, even thrived, because workers and management agreed on a united vision and then dedicated themselves to achieving success. At these companies, the General Electrics, Mercks, Intels, America Online, Inc.'s, and Microsofts of the world, a remarkable level of synergy exists. Employer and employee believe in—and trust—each other.

What, exactly, explains these profound differences?

The Management Tradition

To understand the present, it is essential to examine the past. In *Workplace 2000*, Joseph H. Boyett and Henry P. Conn retrace the history of what they call "the American Management Tradition" by examining the inner workings of corporate organizations.

They note that large organizations were characterized by three classes of employee: the managerial elite, or significant people; a professional tier of middle managers or those with technical skills; and the lower cadre, or *insignificant workers*, whose job was to assemble products and perform generally routine tasks. These individuals were deemed insignificant because these functions could be performed by anyone.[1] This organizational approach was called scientific management. As the authors note:

> The premise behind scientifically designed jobs was that managers, with the help of professionals, could carefully and systematically analyze each task to be performed in the workplace and determine the quickest and best methods of performing the task . . . In the course of designing work, the tasks to be performed would be broken down to their most fundamental level. Workers could then focus on performing one or a few discrete, predefined, and carefully measured acts in the workplace. All associated functions required for designing and coordinating the efforts of the mass of workers would be performed by managers, supervisors, or specialists. Thus, the worker would have no responsibility or input into quality standards.[2]

Indeed, while employees focused on repetitive work, management concentrated on creating greater efficiencies through better work design and using new technologies to increase productivity.

The results were nothing less than impressive. Over the last century, productivity in manufacturing and transportation increased three to four percent annually. As workweeks continued to decrease, time for leisurely activities increased. Time spent at work decreased from an average of 70 hours in the mid-1890s to 39.2 hours in 1996. By 2010, over 50 percent of lifetime activities will consist of leisure time.[3]

In fact, according to Peter Drucker, this revolution in productivity was arguably the most important social event of the last century.[4] The rise in productivity has allowed us to revolutionize our society in myriad ways and build an entire economy based on leisure activities.

Yet, this almost obsessive focus on productivity is not without drawbacks. It translated into employers asserting ever-greater control over how employees did their jobs, while undervaluing human creativity. In turn, this led to greater dissatisfaction among workers and a continuing downward spiral centering on attitudes, feelings, and commitment.

The result? The *insignificant workers* banded together and formed unions to protect their jobs. Consequently, the emerging dynamic of the twentieth century became the interplay between labor and management. In unionized environments, collective bargaining guaranteed a degree of fairness, and sometimes even stability. Negotiations focused on the bread-and-butter issues surrounding pay, benefits, and work rules. When one side wanted new work rules and the other side resisted, strikes or other actions ensued until both sides struck a new balance.

In non-unionized environments, employers struggled to balance the need to remain competitive against the need to preserve stable labor relations. Consequently, many large employers provided pay and benefits similar to or, in some cases, even better than those obtained through the collective bargaining process. The near-universal extension of health and pension benefits to workers in large manufacturing concerns was for the most part driven by the labor movement. Still, the price of labor-management harmony was often less innovation and decreased efficiency.

In large measure, these internal struggles forced corporations to become more inwardly focused. Each became an island of institutional culture that deadened the organizational ability to react to new challenges in the marketplace.

Post-World War II to 1970: Stability in the Workplace

From the end of World War II to the oil shocks of the early 1970s, stability in the marketplace led to stability in the workplace. During this period, management functioned as a purveyor of corporate information, values, and control. The stereotype of the "organization man"—an employee who would do, without question, what the company needed—was widespread. Although more myth than reality, people generally believed that if you "kept your nose clean, you had a job for life." Even during a recession or downturn in sales, many firms balked at handing out pink slips.

Companies like IBM or Delta Airlines, or entire industries such as petroleum, acquired reputations as employers of choice, since those companies never let workers go—a pattern that some preserved well into the 1980s or, in some cases, the 1990s. To be let go branded an individual as a failure. Job applicants who had switched employers one or more times were viewed as disloyal job-hoppers and often rejected out of hand. Workers at all levels built their careers around what the company did. Management succession nearly planned itself, drawing candidates from large pools of seasoned employees who knew the company and carried its culture in their briefcases.

Pay and benefit practices during the post-war period were driven by this labor-management philosophy. Pay schemes, such as the Hay system, valued jobs by assigning points based on internal factors such as skill, effort, and accountability. The idea was to create internal equity across departments and divisions of an organization. This approach to valuing jobs created a predictable framework. Managers used Hay points, based on an employee's level of responsibility and job content, to determine salary or pay. That meant that individuals at the same job classification level received the same compensation, whether or not their jobs actually warranted it. At its height, every Fortune 100 company used Hay points— all with the goal of creating internal equity and consistency.

Benefits also reflected the era of job stability. Health care was usually fully paid by the employer. Retirement benefits were, generally, based on the average of one's career earnings, and were usually paid from *defined benefit plans*. This translated into a specific sum, usually in the form of an annuity, paid out at retirement. Not until the 1970s, as a response to the enormous inflation of the era, did organizations begin using *final pay defined benefit plan* formulas, which base retirement benefits on the average of one's last years of service.

As Figure 1.1 demonstrates, unlike career-based formulas, which were slow to change in the inflationary environment, final pay defined benefit plans allowed retirement benefits to float with wages. Becoming vested in retirement benefits also took a long time. Before the enactment of the Employee Retirement Income Security Act (ERISA) in 1974, it was not uncommon to see plans that required 10 or 20 years of uninterrupted service before a person could qualify for retirement benefits.

As onerous as this might seem today, organizations expected long service and built compensation and retirement policies around

Figure 1.1
Aligning Benefits with Workforce

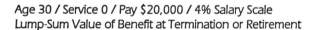

Age 30 / Service 0 / Pay $20,000 / 4% Salary Scale
Lump-Sum Value of Benefit at Termination or Retirement

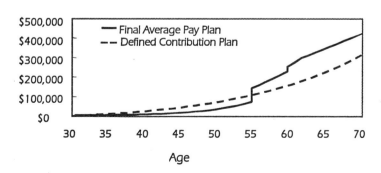

the concept. Job-hopping was severely frowned upon. Those who changed ships too often were viewed as a potential liability, since their loyalty could not be trusted. Portability of benefits was not a significant issue since no one expected to leave. Nevertheless, the seeds of change were in the wind.

1970 to the Mid-1980s: Conglomerates to Merger Mania

The 1970s ushered in the era of the conglomerate. Huge horizontal mergers produced behemoths like General Electric, which today operates in businesses as diverse as financial services, aircraft engine manufacturing, consumer electronics, plastics, lighting, and television broadcasting. Suddenly, size mattered. The career path within these organizations typically included a series of rotational assignments through diverse business units. Instead of creating value, companies focused on acquiring their way to greater worth.

Nonetheless, not everyone accepted the wisdom of such a business philosophy. After Mobil Oil acquired retailing giant Montgomery Ward in 1974, Senator Edward Kennedy expressed his displeasure. He pointed to windfall oil profits as an example of corporate excess and challenged Mobil's claim that it was interested in finding new petroleum reserves. "How much oil do you think they'll find in the aisles of Montgomery Ward?" he quipped.

However, politicians were not the only ones questioning the value of these new organizations. Shareholders began to wonder what exactly was going on. Stocks began to under-perform historical norms. It became glaringly apparent that management at most of these companies could not govern such a diverse set of businesses. They simply did not have the knowledge, expertise, or focus.

A prime example is Eastman Kodak, a company that began assembling a diverse set of businesses, including chemicals and financial services, during the 1970s and 1980s. Only after profits began to sputter did it become apparent that the organization had strayed too far from its photographic roots. It had become bloated and inefficient. Throughout the 1980s and 1990s, having endured restructuring and a series of layoffs—in 1983 Kodak cut 12,900 workers worldwide, then 7,500 in 1988 and 1989—it remained a laggard.

Shareholders and consumers, particularly during the later stages of this era, began to exert a heavy influence on corporate behavior. This pushed the labor-management dialectic to the background, and, as a result, both labor and management suffered. Wealth was transferred from employees to shareholders in the form of increased capital growth, and to consumers in the form of increased product value. Wages stagnated and jobs disappeared, all while middle management became superfluous. The full effect of technology and communications began to take hold.

Figure 1.2
A Decade of Layoffs[5]

Year	U.S. Jobs Lost
1990 (recession year)	315,000
1991 (recession year)	555,000
1992 (recession year)	275,000
1993	625,000
1994	515,000

Mid-1980s to the Present: A New Playing Field

From 1987 through the early 1990s, 85 percent of *Fortune* 1000 firms downsized their white-collar workforces. In 1993, a Watson Wyatt study of 531 companies found that one-fourth had slashed their workforces by more than 20 percent within the prior two years.[6] A 1998 American Management Association survey of 4,500 managers of major U.S. corporations found that 61 percent had seen their current employers eliminate jobs since January 1990. Moreover, 21 percent indicated that their companies employ fewer people today than in 1990.[7]

Obviously, prosperity is no protection against downsizing. As the mid-1990s economic machine produced one of the great booms of history, restructuring droned on. However, downsizing in the '90s began to take on a far different quality: 92 percent of job seekers who had been laid off in 1998 found employment with equivalent or better salaries.[8]

During the 1990s, job cutting became an outgrowth of merger mania, which rippled through almost every industry at an ever-accelerating pace. In 1998, companies announced or completed 23,926 deals worldwide.[9] The value of these mergers reached $2.4 trillion—almost a fivefold increase over 1991.[10] In almost every instance, the avowed purpose of these mergers was consolidation of function and staffs in order to fend off competition.

In reality, most mergers produced negative results. For example, a study of 100 large deals occurring between 1994 and 1997 found that two-thirds resulted in immediate and outright losses to shareholders, while the companies under-performed industry peers over the long haul.[11] Indeed, after all the lofty talk about synergies and efficiencies had died down, the goal of better communication, greater entrepreneurship, greater cooperation, and improved productivity had failed to materialize. Another study found that 82 percent of merged banks saw their stock lag behind that of peers from 1995 to 1998, one of the great bull markets of history.[12]

This upheaval has created an employment environment shrouded in uncertainty and anxiety. For older workers, angst is driven by job insecurity. It takes terminated managers over the age of 55 twice as long to find a job as those under the age of 35.[13] At the same time, younger workers are continually looking for individual growth opportunities that will keep them employable. In the end, no group—or person—seems entirely content.

These attitudes reflect the realities of the labor marketplace, but they also feed into the actions and behaviors of everyone involved. It is no wonder that an American Management Association survey found that downsized managers who join other organizations feel less attached to their new employers.[14]

Figure 1.3
How Workers Feel About Loyalty and Trust

Agreed-Upon Statements About Present Employer	Terminated in Prior Job	Never Terminated
I feel a strong sense of belonging to my organization.	63%	71.7%
This organization has a great deal of personal meaning to me.	53.6%	69.3%
I would be happy to spend the rest of my career with this organization.	51.3%	61.0%
I feel as if this organization's problems are my own.	50.2%	60.3%
I feel like part of the family at my organization.	47.9%	58.2%
I think I could easily become as attached to another organization as I am to this one.	78.9%	42.6%
I do not feel emotionally attached to this organization.	25.9%	19.5%

The impact of this upheaval is not confined to workers who are the victims of downsizing. Of the 1,441 HR managers from companies that reduced their workforces between 1990 and July 1996, nearly three-quarters reported an immediate and negative impact on the surviving employees' morale. The effect still lingered a year later among 36 percent of employees.[15]

Studies consistently show that the majority of restructuring attempts fail to improve productivity and do not lead to better decision making, improved communication, greater entrepreneurship, and greater cooperation. In fact, more often than not, the real outcome of these efforts has been a decline in worker productivity, lower morale, risk aversion, loss of critical skill employees, and lower quality and customer service.[16]

Anxiety about job security continues to plague workers. In a recent survey, workers' apprehension about jobs was three times higher now than during the depths of the 1980-1981 recession. Nearly 25 percent of employed executives indicated their jobs were directly linked to company performance, up from seven percent in the prior year.[17] Employers who trumpeted the new contract and the end of paternalism as part of corporate re-structuring are now reaping what they sowed. The American Management Association survey on "Downsizing, Job Elimination and Job Creation" found notable increases in absenteeism (7 percent), disability claims (10 percent), and turnover (28 percent) among the survivors of downsizing.[18]

Where workers once believed in job security, they now believe in career security. That means keeping up their skills and changing jobs regularly to gain experience and knowledge. In fact, these individuals must sometimes reinvent themselves over the course of their careers, or change a career path in midstream. Today, employability overshadows employment. Self-allegiance blots out commitment. More often than not, cynicism reigns supreme.

The Changing Workplace

Even as mergers and layoffs created eye-catching headlines, more subtle forces were reshaping the face of work. These factors are easily identified: demographics, technology, globalization, and diversity.

Demographics: The Challenge Ahead

The most profound demographic change today is the aging American population. As one publication noted: "By 2025, the proportion of all Americans who are elderly will be the same as the proportion in Florida today . . . America, in effect, will become a nation of Floridas."[19]

The median workforce age is also rising. In 1962, the median age of the American workforce, driven by the late entry of workers after World War II, reached 40.5, its highest modern level. By 1979, the median age had dropped to 34.7 as a result of the baby boom. However, by 2005 the median age of American workers will be back to 40.5.[20]

The impact of baby boomers (the 76 million or so children born in the United States between 1945 and 1964) is inescapable. As they move through each phase of their life cycle, they reshape the workplace like a giant river carving through the topography. In the 1950s, they propelled mass construction of schools; in the 1970s, they swelled the ranks of universities; in the 1980s, they heated up housing prices because of their competition for homes. Now, their children will replay some of the same scenarios. As they age, boomers will not only need new industries and services to address their needs; they will have a defining impact on the workplace.

While aging is an important issue, it does not represent the entire picture. Older workers are now exiting the workplace faster than they can be replaced, and at the historically young age of 62. When baby boomers begin to retire, the baby bust generation (also called Generation X) will be left to take up the slack. Unfortunately, the continuous decline of the worker-to-retiree ratio will put tremendous strain on the future of Social Security. Between 1995 and 2010, the ratio of worker to retiree will be four-to-one, waning to two-to-one by 2030.[21]

Already, the number of younger workers has declined by 14 percent during the 1990s. Meanwhile, the demand for workers, reflected in the growth of the U.S. workforce, has swelled 1.5 to 2 percent per year—or about 15 to 20 percent per decade—over the last 20 years. In the final analysis, that translates into a shortfall of young workers in the years to come.[22] Figure 1.4 illustrates this worker shortfall.

Figure 1.4
Shortage in the Number of Young Workers

Age of Worker	1970 – 1980	1980 – 1990	1996 – 2006
20 – 24	+ 49.8%	- 13.1%	+ 15.6%
25 – 34	+ 71.3%	+ 22.3%	- 8.6%
35 – 44	+ 24.8%	+ 55.1%	- 3.1%

(Demand increasing at 2% per year.)

Economic growth often accompanies labor force growth. However, it is not a two-dimensional equation. Other factors can mask the impact of an expanding labor market. For example, increased productivity can diminish the effect of demographics. The rate of GDP growth during the 1980s matched the prior decade despite fewer new workers. Although fewer bodies were available, a modest improvement in productivity filled the gap.[23] Ultimately, the process feeds on itself. Economic growth leads to greater opportunity, which in turn boosts labor force participation.

Of course, trying to match demographic trends with job availability is a bit like trying to predict the weather. There are simply too many variables involved to get it right all the time, or even some of the time. In addition, the boom and bust nature of business cycles plays a significant role in affecting supply and demand for workers. Poor economic times translate into plenty of workers available at all levels, while periods of rapid economic growth inevitably spell labor shortages. What can be said with certainty is that demographics force changes in who does the work and how they do it.

A case in point is Chevron, one of the world's leading integrated petroleum companies. The numbers tell the tale. Of the firm's 25,500 U.S. employees, more than 15,000 are baby boomers, two-thirds of whom are within a few years of retirement eligibility. Only about 3,000 employees are under age 34. Slower hiring and downsizing over the past decade boosted the average age of the workforce. Chevron's own data suggests that the company could see up to 1,000 retirements annually. The company faces a critical shortage of engineers and support personnel, with the prediction that the problem will worsen over the next five years. This situation led one observer to ask rhetorically, "Through a multitude of individual decisions . . . is it possible for a workforce to downsize the company, instead of the other way around?"[24]

Chevron's situation is not unique. Across industries, the pattern of an aging workforce is likely to be repeated. The problem is twofold: (1) older workforces generally result in higher compensation and benefit costs, and (2) as older workers retire, they leave a knowledge and experience gap in their wake.

Technology

Demography is only one force remaking the workplace. Another is technology. Everyone in the workplace today has witnessed the profound impact of technology. Those over age 40 can recall working in offices that first acquired a copy machine, making carbon paper an instant anachronism. Later came the fax machine, which turned telex machines into dinosaurs. Then came the electric calculator and the computer, which put typewriters and adding machines into the dustbin. Today, it is happening again with wireless communication, networking, and global satellites.

Throughout history, technology has changed the nature of work. In the early 1980s, manager after manager became aware that a newfangled device called a word processor might be a useful addition, but it would also put many secretaries out of work. Although people were frightened by this phenomenon, it soon became apparent that it changed the nature of jobs rather than eliminating them. Dorthea Jones,[25] an elegant, elderly secretary at a *Fortune* 500 company, faced this problem. Although her boss rebuked the office manager who forced the department to use a word processor and put Ms. Jones out of work, the boss did not realize that the woman's knowledge and expertise were valuable assets. Indeed, Ms. Jones eventually became the corporate librarian, and functioned as the "institutional memory" for several years.

Over the last 20 years, the scenario of displaced secretaries has played in offices all across the globe. Today, executives use word processing software to create their own letters and documents, a profound change from the way work was performed in decades past. Like many technologies, word processing changed not only the way people work, but also how they think about work.

Today, technology fosters change at a staggering pace. In 1965, Gordon E. Moore, the cofounder of Intel, proposed what has come to be termed "Moore's Law." Moore's Law states that the number of transistors that researchers can pack on a single microchip doubles every eighteen months. Chips that could hold 65,000 transistors in the 1970s have been eclipsed by semiconductors able to support 125 million transistors today.[26]

Figure 1.5
Moore's Law

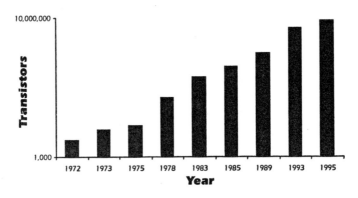

As the pace of technology has accelerated, prices of hardware and software have fallen dramatically, making new information technology widely available. In 1975, a $10 million IBM mainframe could process 10 million instructions per second. Today, an ordinary desktop Pentium computer is about 40 times faster and costs only $2,000. The capital cost of performing one million instructions was $1 million in 1975 compared to $45 in 1995. To bring this price revolution into perspective, it is as if a Rolls Royce costing $100,000 in 1975 would cost $4.50 in 1995![27]

The communications revolution also has redefined the nature of work. In today's workplace, communication is constant, and almost instantaneous. E-mail has replaced the office memo. The Internet and internal Intranets allow companies to leverage their global reach in ways that were unfathomable only a decade ago. Work moves around the globe on an around-the-clock basis, document and project revisions occur instantaneously, and people can be reached anywhere, anytime.

The effect of fewer employees and advanced communications is a radical shift in the ratio of chiefs to tribesmen. Today, fewer chiefs are necessary, and flatter organizations can perform more quickly and efficiently than the bloated, hierarchical companies of the past. With this heightened ability—and need—to communicate, organizations are no longer constrained by space and time. A huge, central headquarters is a liability rather than an asset. Decentralized work becomes a strategic advantage rather than a necessary evil. The U.S. Department of Labor predicts that by 2002, telecommuters will constitute ten percent of the workforce. Many analysts believe that number is conservative.[28] Likewise, the Internet is revolutionizing client interaction, leading one futurist to predict that by 2007 all business-to-business sales will be conducted over the Internet, while 25 percent of retail sales will occur online.[29]

Today, companies look to technology to streamline processes. Not long ago, Federal Reserve Chairman Alan Greenspan noted that " . . . the newer technologies have made capital investment distinctly more profitable, enabling firms to substitute capital for labor far more productively than they could have a decade or two ago."[30] Indeed, technology has made it possible for corporations to return to their core businesses and outsource administrative functions to specialized vendors.

Displacement might sound like a dirty word, but the net result of technology in the workplace has been dramatically positive. One recent study attributes 30 percent to 50 percent of the demand for skilled workers over the past 25 years to computers.[31] In the beginning, the income gains associated with these jobs fell into the eager hands of the well-educated and the elite. Now it is clear that the benefits of the technology boom reach all workers.[32] In 1999, the *Times* of London observed that the United States has enjoyed low unemployment, low inflation, and low interest rates as a direct result of the vast investment in computers and communications technology.[33]

Today's emerging digital economy, and the resulting emphasis on knowledge workers, is also changing the way young people prepare for the workplace. In 1997, a staggering 67 percent of U.S. high school graduates went to college, compared to 49 percent in 1979. The proportion of society between the ages of 25 and 29 who have an undergraduate degree has increased from 21.3 percent in 1981 to a record 27.8 percent in 1997. Meanwhile, the skilled worker crunch is leading employers to expand training opportunities for employees.[34] Employers see that technology, once the scourge of labor, might transform the twenty-first century into the Golden Age of Labor.

In the end, the challenge of technological growth is not the technology itself, which constantly forces organizations to adopt new tools and retrain workers. It is teaching people to use hardware and software to boost the bottom line and eliminate inefficiencies. The "old dog" corporations must learn new tricks or find themselves nudged aside by smarter dogs who have no habits of unwanted knowledge to unlearn.

Globalization of the Workforce

Closely linked to the growth of technology is globalization. One recent survey shows that 41 percent of corporate revenues for U.S.-based multinationals are generated outside headquarters.[35] As the U.S. economy continues to send ripples throughout the world, it becomes intertwined with other economies and cultures. All at once, American workers must tend to international customers and co-workers. They must learn new customs so that they can interact seamlessly with foreign-based counterparts.

Today, workers from every corner of the world are drawn into the global marketplace. Some move physically closer to the work. Others link to the marketplace through telephones, modems, and Web browsers. The virtual workplace—one in which information passes back and forth without regard to physical boundaries and borders—is quickly becoming the foundation for twenty-first century work. Best-of-class companies, such as Intel, Hewlett Packard, and IBM, offer cross-cultural training to managers and staff who work on multicultural teams.

The acceleration toward a global economy is staggering. In 1965, less than four percent of jobs were linked to foreign trade. In 2000, 25 percent of all manufacturing jobs are export-related. By 2010, nearly 50 percent of all U.S. manufacturing jobs will be export-related.[36] During the debate on the North American Free Trade Agreement (NAFTA), a newscaster visited rural South Carolina expecting to find opposition to the United States dropping trade barriers with neighbors. Instead of opposition, he found farmers who raised tobacco for trade in foreign markets, and workers whose factories sold the products abroad. Almost uniformly, they believed that free trade represented more of an opportunity than a threat to their economic well-being.

It is Economics 101. When prosperity rises, so does the demand for new workers. In the United States, immigration of highly skilled workers has become critical to maintaining productivity. In addition, immigrants eager to embrace the American way of life are drawn by stories of success and high wages. Immigration is having a profound effect on the nation's workforce demographics. While in the 1980s immigration accounted for 25 percent of workforce growth, it accounted for 50 percent of the growth in the 1990s.[37]

Globalization changes the workplace in important ways:

◆ A new employee base will enter the workforce, located in the United States and outside of the United States.

◆ U.S.-based employees will need to learn new, culturally sensitive ways to approach situations.

◆ Managers must assess employees in order to understand how cultural differences affect motivation, rewards, and performance.

◆ Products and services will change as a result of the meshing of cultures.

Diversity

Without question, the demographic and political landscape has changed dramatically since the mid-1980s, when researchers at the Hudson Institute first presented the business case for a diverse workforce. As seers looking into a crystal ball, analysts predicted massive changes in the complexion of the workforce. Companies would continue to seek women, minorities, and immigrants. Indeed, as the demographics of the United States underwent fundamental change, the composition of the workforce would reflect society. Clearly, the seers did not expect the economic boom of the 1990s. At present, shortages exist for all types of labor, and chronic shortages exist within selected occupations. This enormous demand, particularly in technical and professional fields, means that companies must increasingly hire people from divergent backgrounds.

Nevertheless, the notion of diversity is still treated as a corporate value rather than an irreversible outcome of economic trends. Valuing diversity as an intrinsic good masks a more fundamental need. Companies that screen talent based on what that talent looks like—the age, the gender, the ethnicity—are not only confronted with growing legal battles. Their very existence is threatened because they do not have an adequate labor pool to handle the work.

The real diversity issue is not about tolerating differences among workers. It is also not about affirmatively hiring people of different backgrounds to guarantee a mix of employees. Instead, it is about finding the talent to fuel a demanding global economy and then retaining the right people. Economic necessity, not an edifice of laws and social conventions, now forces employers to pursue these skills regardless of age, color, gender, sexual preference, or ethnic origin. Indeed, the challenge for the new millennium is learning to integrate individuals of different backgrounds, languages, attitudes, and needs into a single, cohesive corporate culture.

Conclusion

Today's organization—particularly human resources departments—must recognize that it is impossible to turn to the past for simple answers. The employer-employee relationship has undergone fundamental change over the last quarter century, while technology has opened the frontiers of global business. It is no longer possible to build an outstanding workforce insulated by language, culture, or religion. The quest for skilled employees and knowledge workers knows no geographic or political boundaries.

The new human resources challenge is understanding that even the best business strategy will fail without the right people to execute it. In an era of labor shortages, skyrocketing demand for products, and global technology, the answer increasingly lies in diversity. Today, skills and knowledge are the currency of corporate success. Attracting and retaining the right people is a necessity. Ultimately, it is human capital that drives a company toward world-class status.

Notes

[1] Joseph H. Boyett and Henry P. Conn, *Workplace 2000: The Revolution Reshaping American Business* (New York: NAL, 1992).

[2] Ibid.

[3] Graham T.T. Molitor, "Trends and Forecasts for the New Millennium," *The Futurist*, September 1, 1998.

[4] Peter Drucker, *Managing for the Future* (New York: Saint Martin Press, 1993).

[5] Ronald B. Morgan, Jack E. Smith (contributor), *Staffing the New Workplace: Selecting and Promoting for Quality Improvement* (New York: ASQ Quality Press, 1996).

[6] "Best Practices in Corporate Restructuring," Watson Wyatt Worldwide survey, 1995.

[7] "Career Advancement in the 1990s," American Management Association survey, 1998.

[8] Daniel McGinn and John McCormick, "Your Next Job," *Newsweek,* February 1, 1999, p. 45.

[9] Gretchen Morgenson, "A Cautionary Note on Mergers: Bigger Does Not Mean Better," *New York Times*, December 8, 1998.

[10] "Making Mergers Work," *The Economist*, January 9, 1999.

[11] Gretchen Morgenson.

[12] Gretchen Morgenson.

[13] Eric Rolfe Greenberg, "AMA Research: Downsizing and the Career Path," *HRfocus*, March 1998.

[14] Eric Rolfe Greenberg.

[15] "Survey on Downsizing, Job Elimination and Job Creation," American Management Association survey, 1996.

[16] Ronald B. Morgan, Jack E. Smith.

[17] Beth Belton, "Despite Humming Economy, Workers Sweat Job Security," *USA Today*, March 2, 1999.

[18] "Survey on Downsizing, Job Elimination and Job Creation," American Management Association survey, 1996.

[19] Peter G. Peterson, "Will America Grow up Before It Grows Old?" *Atlantic Monthly*, May 1996, 277(5): 55.

[20] Ronald E. Kutscher, "The American Workforce: 1992-2005", Bulletin 2452, U.S. Department of Labor, April 1994, p. 3.

[21] Richard W. Judy and Carol D'Amico, *Workforce 2020: Work and Workers in the 21st Century* (Indianapolis: Hudson Institute, Inc., 1997).

[22] "Demographics & Destiny: Winning the War for Talent," Watson Wyatt Worldwide survey, 1998.

[23] Ronald E. Kutscher.

[24] Jay Stuller, "The Renewal," *Chevron Now*, July 1998.

[25] Dorthea Jones is a fictional name representing a real person.

[26] Richard W. Judy, Carol D'Amico.

[27] Richard W. Judy, Carol D'Amico.

[28] Richard W. Judy, Carol D'Amico.

[29] Joan Lloyd, "Changing Workplace: Technology Continues to Spark New Workplace Ideas, Trends," Milwaukee *Journal Sentinel*, February 7, 1999.

[30] Beth Belton, *USA Today*, March 2, 1999.

[31] "The 21st Century Economy: The Human Factor, Wages," *Business Week*, August 31, 1998, p. 72.

[32] Ibid.

[33] Roger Bootle, "One American Miracle at a Time," The *Times* of London, February 22, 1999.

[34] *Business Week*, p. 72.

[35] "Global Relocation Trends 1999 Survey Report", Windham International, National Foreign Trade Council (NFTC), Institute for International Human Resources (IIHR).

[36] Richard W. Judy, Carol D'Amico.

[37] Richard W. Judy, Carol D'Amico.

chapter

Human Resources and the Bottom Line

After completing this chapter, you should be able to:

- ◆ Understand the changes in workplace commitment.
- ◆ Realize why trust is important and find ways to establish it.
- ◆ Understand why empowered decision making creates engagement.
- ◆ Define the new role of HR in business planning.
- ◆ Recognize the qualities that lead to success.

"People are our competitive advantage."

"Our employees make our company distinctly different—and superior."

"We value our human capital."

Today, these words are uttered with an almost religious fervor. Management teams across the globe recite these statements, print them on posters, plaster them on training materials, and proceed to make them the centerpiece of their strategy to become a "world-class" organization. Unfortunately, the words often ring hollow. Words alone do not translate into financial and organizational performance. It's simply not enough for a company to say that it values its people; it must demonstrate their worth every day, and in every way.

A company must humbly recognize that even the greatest ideas and products do not necessarily translate into success and profits. History is littered with the debris of great ideas that never became viable business concepts. In fact, it is people who transform an organization from ordinary to superior. It is people who ring up sales and cement relationships with customers. Human capital, and the human resources department that helps shape a workforce and its culture, ultimately have a significant impact on the bottom line. Understanding this simple but profound fact, and finding ways to measure and reward employees, is the centerpiece of a successful human resources strategy.

The Loss of Trust

As the traditional employee/employer relationship has changed, the way that companies go about the business of handling human resources has changed, too. The decline of the paternal corporation, while positive in many respects, has inexorably tilted the power structure of the modern organization. It has brought forth ramifications and implications that would have been impossible to imagine only a decade or two ago. As one author notes:

> Since the late 1960s, Americans have lost faith in virtually all established institutions, including some that had previously been seen as sources of personal economic security. Among the latter are not only corporations but also labor unions, whose fall from grace is apparent in polling data and in a steady decline in the proportion of American workers who belong to unions. Nor is this loss of faith a peculiarly American phenomenon. Declining

respect for hierarchical authority in general, and government in particular, is a global trend characteristic of most advanced industrialized nations.[1]

As trust has shrunk, individualism has grown. As workers have lost faith in their organization's ability to protect them, their need to protect themselves has pushed to the forefront of their consciousness. Over the last quarter century, the American workplace has become a place of expanding rights and declining responsibilities. Legislation and litigation have pervaded every avenue of the work environment. Benefit rights have been augmented. The courts have continually expanded the concept of privacy rights. Willingness to participate and sacrifice for the greater good is less apparent today than in times past.

The corporate world has fostered the move to increased individual focus by backing away from its previous commitment to career employment. However, this swing in the other direction has created an entirely different set of problems. "What's in it for me?" has become a knee-jerk response to new corporate initiatives. While some might argue that this is a fairer, less oppressive situation than in times past, Frederick Reichheld, author of *The Loyalty Effect*, offers compelling evidence that lost loyalty can have destructive results on employees and on customers.

> Most companies lose half of their employees in three-to-four years, and half of their customers in five . . . Retaining employees is as critical as retaining customers because you won't have loyal customers without loyal employees.[2]

In one survey, employees admitted that they were aware of a negative impact on their work when they experienced a decline in loyalty. They worked only the required number of hours, lost focus more easily, and missed deadlines. On the other hand, employees who are committed to their companies are willing to work harder, take on extra projects, and take greater pride in their accomplishments. Surveys show a direct link between employee loyalty and customer retention, productivity, customer satisfaction, and increased sales.[3]

Rebuilding Trust

How does an organization rebuild trust and commitment? Certainly, managers don't expect to recreate the same kind of allegiance that existed in the 1960s, '70s, and '80s. Today's workers are savvy enough to recognize that it's not a good idea to place blind trust in leaders or faithfully back every new vision. The experience of the last 20 years—a period marked by major restructurings—has shattered the idea of career employment. The newspaper headlines and television commercials regarding corporate commitment remain indelibly etched on our shared consciousness.

The truth is, nobody wants to return to the past. Today's global marketplace requires quick decision making in response to ever-changing conditions. The large, layered institutions of the past would be too slow to compete. What's more, information technology simply doesn't allow the luxury of retaining the same jobs, skills, and processes over a period of years. The workplace of the new millennium is one of constant change and flux. It is a dynamic organism that is forced to reinvent itself in months, not years.

Today, people increasingly create information and ideas rather than hard goods. The percentage of workers who produce and deliver nonprofessional services such as food service, lodging, distribution, retail, and beauty services has declined from 83 percent of the workforce in 1900 to an estimated 41 percent in 2000. At the same time, the percentage of workers dealing with information (sales, management, professional services, and clerical work) has increased from 17 percent to 59 percent in the same period.[4] The individuals who engage in these types of activities require different incentives and methods of leadership.

Ultimately, recreating trust and commitment centers on empowering people to make appropriate decisions. It's important to recognize that a highly centralized model of decision making can overemphasize internal information while ignoring obvious problems, concerns, and market issues apparent to those on the front lines. However, pushing decision making too far down in the organization can result in an unfocused approach and a fuzzy notion of what strategy is necessary. Today, decisions must be made close to the facts, but high enough within the organization that internal factors such as corporate goals, economics, and risks are factored into the equation. As one researcher noted:

> The contribution of even a highly skilled and motivated workforce will be limited if jobs are structured, or programmed, in such a way that employees, who presumably know their work better than anyone else, do not have the opportunity to use their skills and abilities to design new and better ways of performing their roles.[5]

Driving Success Through Empowered Decision Making

Steve Bookbinder, a noted workforce consultant, asserts that the modern workplace must be one that offers a sense of purpose and responsibility. He notes:

> As employees take more responsibility and control in their jobs, their sense of satisfaction and motivation increases. At the same time, their acceptance of more responsibility heightens their expectation that they will have the opportunity to demonstrate their capabilities and be rewarded for their contributions.[6]

Unfortunately, the opposite is too often true. Consider one company that sought to standardize its internal decision-making process. It dutifully hired consultants who trained corporate executives to provide all the information necessary to make a given decision on an 8½- by 11-inch piece of paper. The executive making the decision could review the background, the alternatives, the implications, and the recommendation from the single sheet of paper known as a "landscape."

Unfortunately, this method only served to entrench decision making by senior executives who were too far away from the facts. A better approach would have been to empower lower-level executives with decision-making authority and then hold them accountable for their actions. The employees would have been happier and felt more valued, and, in all likelihood, the final decision would have been more on target.

The National Football League's initial use of "instant replay" to support the decisions of referees further illustrates the problem with centralized decision making. Whenever a team protested a penalty call or the referees were unsure, the game stopped so that a referee sitting in the press box could review videotape. Knowing that the play was subject to review, the referees stopped relying on their instinct and began making a greater number of erroneous calls. Adding to the problem: the spike in calls requiring review began to cause delays and affect the sport adversely. In the end, the league suspended the review procedure altogether.*

The NFL example is classic. When decisions are subject to review or when the appropriate individual with the competence to make decisions lacks the authority, commitment wanes. Decisions travel "up the ladder," resulting in poorer quality decisions and an enormous amount of wasted time. But perhaps the most significant negative outcome is risk aversion. In a bureaucracy, the higher in the organization a decision takes place, the more conservative it is. Yet, taking prudent risks is what successful business is predicated on. It opens new markets and creates new and often better ways of producing, marketing, or selling.

Empowering employees to act isn't a new idea. However, while people laud the firms who actively empower their workforce, few put it into practice. A recent Watson Wyatt Worldwide survey of over 9,000 employees from all job levels and from a wide variety of industries found that only 47 percent of employees said that they are encouraged to take risks on the job. Even fewer, 27 percent, said that they were involved in the decisions that affect them. And only 30 percent felt that their companies treated them as valued business partners.[7]

Empowerment, by its nature, suggests trust: trust that employees have the depth to make the right decisions and trust that management knows what it is doing and that it has the best interests of the employee at heart. Management must trust that employees will use the authority to make decisions for the good of the company. Employees must be held accountable for the decisions they make.

* In 1999, the NFL instituted a revised review procedure.

Ultimately, a delicate balance exists between accountability and the need to take prudent risks. In order to encourage employees to make decisions and take appropriate risks, they must believe that the organization will not usually judge them on individual decisions as much as overall outcomes and performance. Under such a model, some decisions simply don't work out. But it's a small price to pay to gain total trust. And without trust, engagement isn't possible.

Creating Engagement

Engagement takes commitment one step further by suggesting that the individual is an active participant in furthering organizational goals. Engagement shouldn't be confused with alignment. Engagement signals a willingness to contribute, while alignment ensures that the contribution is consistent with the organization's goals. Getting employees engaged is the key to creating a successful organization. As Figure 2.1 shows, positive engagement yields tangible results.

Figure 2.1
Shareholder Return by Employee Engagement

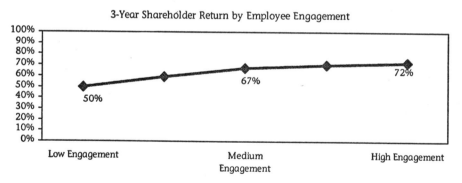

3-Year Shareholder Return by Employee Engagement

What's the best way to engage a workforce? Most companies start by outlining the corporate mission and objectives. They then move to rules of operation based on identified corporate values. Typically, mission, objectives, and values are developed at executive off-site meetings that focus on team building and creating shared corporate and personal values. Employee meetings rally the troops around the new values. Unfortunately, in far too many organizations, this is where it all ends. And the assumption that communication alone can engage workers becomes a recipe for disaster.

At many organizations struggling to attract and retain qualified employees, the focus invariably is on pay. The typical comment is: "We are underpaying our employees. Tell us how much we need to increase pay and benefits to get them to stay." Initially, many of these executives bristle at the notion that their workforce isn't properly engaged, and that the problem is more one of commitment than dollars. Only after considerable analysis and discussion does it become obvious that engagement is indeed the problem. Tossing money at the problem only wastes valuable corporate assets.

Creating engagement in today's marketplace starts with the recognition that it is impossible to predict the future based on the past. Gone is the era in which hierarchical organizations treated their employees as conscripts or children who need to be controlled. Instead, the new employee/employer relationship rests on two decisions: the *decision to produce* and the *decision to participate.*

It's nothing short of quid pro quo. The employee produces something, a widget or a service, and the corporation pays the employee in return. The transaction is discrete; the company knows what it wants and it directs the employee to provide it. When production takes place, remuneration is paid and the process continues. The decision to produce is controlled by the employer, and failure to produce means termination. In this environment an employer gets, as the saying goes, "what it pays for." However, while production is a necessary condition for existence, it generally is not sufficient for achieving success.

Competition challenges the traditional decision to produce by demanding greater productivity. However, the ways to achieve productivity growth are limited. New technology or better production methods can increase output marginally. The biggest gains come from getting employees to work harder or smarter, or both. This requires not just production, but also contribution and participation.

While the decision to produce is in the hands of the employer, the decision to participate belongs to the employee. The ultimate requirement for success is finding a way to ratchet up employee contribution—a particularly difficult challenge in today's tight labor market.

The keys to creating engagement are:[8]

◆ Have a clear mission that drives everything the organization does.

◆ Offer meaningful work and put people's competence and knowledge to work.

◆ Provide training, and let veterans train newcomers.

◆ Allow employees high involvement in setting their performance goals, decisions affecting their work, and the organization's goals.

◆ Build in accountability and review performance against preset objectives.

The point about accountability has far-reaching implications. Not only does the individual need to be held accountable for performance, an organization needs to be held accountable for reinforcing its own values. That means rewarding individuals for doing exactly what the company says it values—whether it's customer service, sales, productivity, innovation, or something else. Keep in mind, however, that these goals must be consistent with the corporate mission and objectives. And everyone, not just rank-and-file workers, must reinforce the concept.

This notion of reciprocal accountability—both employer and employee having a separate but related set of risks and responsibilities—creates engagement. Instead of the expectation of a "job for life" in exchange for hard work, the pact now states that employees will receive a promise of greater rewards, better opportunities, and more input into decisions in exchange for continued loyalty. Employees now expect their employers to live up to their end of the bargain. As one study noted:

> They waited out the bad years—surviving the cutbacks and anxiety—and helped turn things around. Now, not unreasonably, they expect to share in the results of the turnaround. They've taken in all the messages their companies have been communicating about paying for performance; about new opportunities for career growth; about new kinds of mentoring and coaching; about success sharing. But the fact that real sharing hasn't yet materialized—at least not in ways meaningful to employees—is beginning to erode their faith in management and their belief that the workplace is a genuine meritocracy . . .[9]

Reciprocity is the core of any contract, including the unwritten employment contract governing employer/employee expectations. We will discuss this notion in greater detail in a later chapter. For now it is sufficient to observe that in changing messages, we also changed expectations. Unfortunately, management generally gets poor marks in this area. A recent Watson Wyatt Worldwide survey indicated that less than half of the employees who responded rated their managers or supervisors good at the following critical leadership skills:[10]

◆ Encouraging teamwork (51 percent)

◆ Helping solve job-related problems (44 percent)

◆ Helping make time for training and development (42 percent)

◆ Facilitating work group discussions (36 percent)

◆ Coaching (33 percent)

Connecting People to the Bottom Line: The New Role of Human Resources

It is widely accepted that HR can be a source of sustained competitive advantage for businesses. As one observer noted:

> There is a growing consensus in the media that personnel policies can provide a source of competitive advantage. Although there are differences as to what constitutes good practice, many analysts believe that it can improve productivity and, consequently, performance by enhancing skills, promoting positive attitudes and giving people more responsibility so that they can make the fullest use of those skills.[11]

For HR to bolster the bottom line, though, it's essential to meet four basic requirements:

1. HR must add value to the firm's production processes; i.e., levels of individual performance must matter.

2. HR skills must be unique and rare.

3. The combined human capital investments represented by the firm's employees cannot be easily copied or imitated.

4. Technological advances or other substitutes cannot easily replace employees.

While these prerequisites outline the circumstances in which employee talent can make a difference, they don't go far enough in suggesting how to tap into talent to build a business.

Traditionally, human resource functions have been composed of four elements: labor relations, policy design, organizational effectiveness, and administration. These elements were designed to:

♦ Ensure equitable treatment of similarly situated employees.

♦ Manage performance, succession, and organization design.

♦ Provide employee security regarding health, life, and retirement benefits.

♦ Establish and communicate corporate values.

♦ Establish and retain labor peace.

♦ Administer pay/benefit programs and policies.

Because of the growing recognition that human resources plays a strategic role in business planning, HR professionals must understand how to give the company exactly what it needs. The strategic role for human resources falls into three basic areas: hiring, wiring, and retiring. The types of ongoing and periodic programs that support these basic functions are depicted in Figure 2.2.

Figure 2.2
The Human Resources Paradigm

Hiring or recruiting the right people is central to building a successful organization. Organizations need to build profiles that fit with the kind of people who are or will be successful within the organization. Armed with a profile, HR professionals must constantly search for people who match corporate needs. Employing the right people enables a company to pull away from the pack.

Wiring is the second critical function for human resources. It consists of engaging employees to further the business strategy and manage performance on an ongoing basis. Performance management systems must hold people accountable for their performance against clearly identified goals. In the end, promoting and rewarding strong performers for doing what the company needs builds reciprocity into the employment relationship.

Contrary to popular belief, weeding out poor performers is not necessarily negative, as long as it is done fairly and consistently. When employees are incapable of meeting the demands of their job, they place a burden on others and cause internal friction. As long as managers handle separations fairly and in a dignified manner, employees understand the need for the performance process to work on both ends of the spectrum.

Retiring is about transition. In many cases the transition is to another job or to retirement. Part of HR's role is to design plans and programs to mesh with the period in which they want employees to move to retirement status. Too often companies maintain retirement and health plans that encourage workers to leave at the wrong time. As the labor shortage drones on, employers will find themselves challenged to design programs that encourage older workers to stay on the job.

By focusing on these primary functions, HR can build a workforce plan that identifies staffing needs and future sources of employees. It can then ask the questions: *What kinds of occupations will be needed in the future? Who will possess the requisite skills? Where will we find these people?* And it will be able to ferret out answers before designing programs to hire, wire, and retire.

Successful organizations of the future, more than ever, will need to rely on talented, experienced workers. In the past, companies could take raw individuals fresh out of high school or college and mold them to the skills necessary for success. The rate of business innovation and fluctuation has shortened the time horizon for employee development. Just like the rushing of talent to the major leagues, decried by old-time baseball fans, companies too face the need to bring employee skills to bear quickly. Experience not found on hand has to be obtained from the marketplace. Knowing what you need and where to find it puts an organization one step ahead of its competitors.

Understanding the impact of demographics on an organizational structure is also critical to designing effective HR programs. For example, during the 1980s and early '90s, many employers terminated large segments of their workforce. Since large-scale involuntary terminations are nearly always accompanied by a hiring freeze, the result is that these companies find themselves with an older workforce at a time when younger workers are becoming scarcer. In most situations, employers would be better served to maintain a balance appropriate for their businesses between younger workers and more experienced older workers.

As noted in Chapter **one**, Chevron is among the companies that have been caught in the cross hairs of an aging baby boom workforce. Nearly 60 percent of its current U.S. dollar-paid employee population is advancing toward retirement. Because of downsizing in the early 1990s and a hiring slowdown, the average age of Chevron's workforce has steadily risen. As a result, roughly two-thirds of this group has passed retirement age or is within a few years of eligibility. The corporation responded by asking all departments to develop strategic staffing plans to address the issue.[12] More aggressive college recruiting, availability of work and family programs, and flexible work schedules for employees at all ages are part of the corporate prescription. Retaining selected older workers as mentors for younger employees is also on the drawing board. Importantly, the company is struggling to shift management's image of employees as an expense, developed during years of cost cutting, to seeing people as an asset, requiring positive management and investment for the company to thrive.[13]

In the end, a workforce analysis must identify the current situation and what kind of workforce the company needs to be successful. Once such a gap has been identified, employers can develop a strategy to find and retain the right workers.

Measuring Success

Smart companies realize that relying solely on financial indicators does not automatically lead to success, or does focusing on operational measures related to internal processes. Baseball icon Yogi Berra once said, "You can observe a lot by watching." In other words, if managing a firm's talent is critical to its success, then measuring performance against goals is crucial. You have to measure what you want to achieve. Successful companies know how to draw success from their people. They effectively:

♦ Communicate downward,

♦ Promote upward communication,

♦ Encourage innovation,

♦ Foster teamwork across work groups or departments, and

♦ Involve and engage employees.[14]

This proposition has been further validated by various academic studies:

> . . . prior empirical work has consistently found that use of effective human resource management practices enhances firm performance. Specifically, extensive recruitment, selection, and training procedures; formal information sharing, attitude assessment, job design, grievance procedures, and labor-management participation programs; and performance appraisal, promotion, and incentive compensation systems that recognize and reward employee merit have all been widely linked with valued firm-level outcomes. These policies and procedures have been labeled High Performance Work Practices (U.S. Department of Labor, 1993) . . . [15]

A more thorough study conducted by Mark Huselid[16] of Rutgers University confirmed that investments in these High Performance

Work Practices are associated with lower employee turnover, greater productivity, and corporate financial performance. At companies he studied, the gain on a per-employee basis was significant; it amounted to $27,044 more in sales, $18,641 in market value, and $3,814 more in profits. The impact of these work practices on corporate financial performance is in part due to their influence on employee turnover and productivity.

Research has gone farther in demonstrating the link between specific human resource practices and financial success. Watson Wyatt Worldwide developed the "Human Capital Index," or "HCI," to measure human resource management. Using a broad-based survey of 405 publicly traded firms, researchers found that firms that had higher HCI scores indicating better human capital management also did better financially over the short and long terms. Even more interesting was finding an apparent connection between some 30 or so specific human resource practices and financial success. These practices were grouped into five broad categories:

- ◆ Recruiting excellence,

- ◆ Collegial, flexible workplace,

- ◆ Clear rewards and accountability,

- ◆ Communications integrity, and

- ◆ Prudent use of resources.

The last category, "Prudent use of resources," which subsumed a variety of standard training and reward practices, was in fact negatively linked to financial performance. Surveyed companies that engaged in these practices were associated with poorer financial results.[17] We will discuss some of the more specific findings of this research later in the book.

Watson Wyatt Worldwide research also suggests that a positive work climate (the psychological environment within which a group

Figure 2.3
How the Work Climate Affects
Key Performance Factors

Impact of Work Climate
Across 27 manufacturing plants, the more positive scores were on these
work climate factors, the higher the site's annual attendance figures.

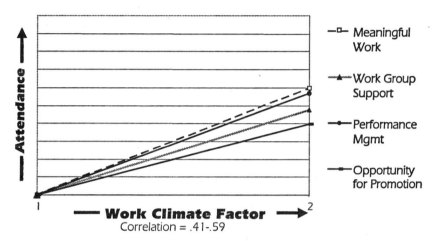

Correlation = .41-.59

operates) affects absenteeism and productivity. When, for example, we examined employee opinion survey results from 27 manufacturing sites within one company, we found that eight factors (respect, meaningful work, use of work groups, openness, supervisor's performance, performance management, recognition, opportunity for advancement) emerged from the analysis as correlated with their overall annual attendance rate. The more positive scores were on these work climate factors, the higher the site's annual attendance figures. In organizations with a poor work climate, the incidence of occupational and non-occupational disability, as well as incidental sickness absence, are much higher than in settings that effectively engage employees.

In recognition of the link between performance and specific practices, Robert S. Kaplan and David P. Norton developed what has come to be known as the "balanced scorecard." It measures key elements of a company's strategy from four different perspectives:

1. Financial performance.

2. Customer knowledge.

3. Internal business processes.

4. Learning and growth.

The authors acknowledge that the ability to achieve success in the financial, customer, and internal business process arenas depends on the company's ability to learn and grow. This ability comes from three sources: employees, systems, and organizational alignment. Employee satisfaction, productivity, and retention are the critical measures of organizational learning and growing. Measures of employee retention and productivity are in many ways a function of employee satisfaction. Satisfied employees are often the critical factor separating bottom-line success from financial failure. In fact, employers who score the highest on employee satisfaction surveys tend to have the greatest number of satisfied customers.

And what exactly does satisfaction mean in the context of the workplace? It's about giving a workforce greater autonomy and involving people in decision making. It's about providing employees with access to sufficient information to do their job well. It means providing recognition for a job well done. And it's all about keeping a workforce connected and enthusiastic about company objectives. Simply put, a workforce that believes in the company and views its contribution as meaningful will achieve far greater success.

In order to keep up with the fast-changing marketplace, an organization must recognize three critical "drivers" or "enablers":

◆ Reskilling of the workforce;

◆ Information system capabilities; and

◆ Motivation, empowerment, and alignment.

In sum, as Kaplan and Norton note:

The balanced scorecard . . . is well suited to the kind of organization many companies are trying to become. The scorecard puts strategy and vision, not control, at the center. It establishes goals but assumes that people will adopt whatever behaviors and take whatever actions are necessary to arrive at those goals. The measures are designed to pull people toward the overall vision. Senior managers may know what the end result should be, but they cannot tell employees exactly how to achieve that result, if only because the conditions in which employees operate are constantly changing.[18]

How does such an approach to management appear at ground zero? In the groundbreaking article, "The Employee-Customer-Profit Chain at Sears,"[19] Anthony Rucci, Steven Kirn, and Richard Quinn chronicled the transformation of Sears, Roebuck and Company from a stodgy retailer with declining market presence to a company on the move, with improving financial re-

Figure 2.4
How Sears Delivered Results[20]

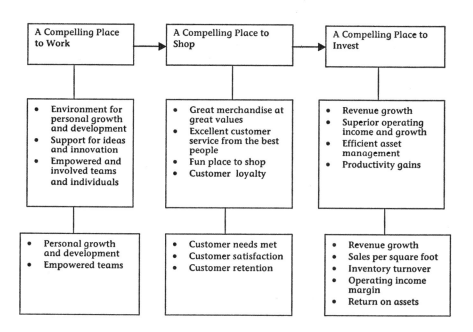

sults and growing customer satisfaction. This radical transformation came about by linking employee behavior to the company's financial performance.

Sears' turnaround strategy focused on making the company a compelling place to work, a compelling place to shop, and finally, a compelling place to invest. Each of these elements of the strategy subsumed its own objectives and measures. What was critical in all this was the recognition that making Sears a compelling place to work meant that as employee attitudes improved, so did the customer experience and financial performance.

Based on internal company research, Sears developed the metrics for identifying financial performance drivers. The model demonstrated that a 5-point improvement in employee attitudes leads to a 1.3-point improvement in customer satisfaction, which in turn leads to a 0.5-percent improvement in revenue growth.

Those are significant results—especially if you consider that the bottom-line benefit to Sears totals tens of millions of dollars a year. Obviously, happy employees were more likely to please customers, who in turn boosted sales. While such an approach doesn't immunize a company from its business cycle, it does put the employee in a position to monitor oncoming economic weather and determine how best to deal with it.

Conclusion

Autonomy. Responsibility. Engagement. The three concepts fit together like hand and glove. People are an organization's source of sustained competitive advantage. And without the right value system and culture, success is as elusive as a desert mirage. In every instance, world-class organizations understand that:

> . . . the elimination of management layers, made possible by information technology and made necessary by intensified competition, has gone hand in hand with decentralization and increased diffusion of decision-making autonomy and responsibility to employees below the man-

agement level. Managers are thus having to make the transition from a command-and-control style of management to a coaching/teamwork style. Meanwhile workers are being asked to concentrate on satisfying customers and, in the process, to think in terms of "the big picture" of the enterprise, rather than one small piece of it.[21]

Engaging employees in their work requires a new kind of leadership. Managing in today's world is not about control. It *is* about creating a framework around a business strategy and identifying each person's expected contribution to the organization. The basic building blocks of success start with understanding who you need and recruiting the right people. In the next chapter we will discuss how to establish the connection between a business's strategy and its people, and how to keep employees aligned with that strategy.

Notes

1 Marina v. N. Whitman, *New World, New Rules: The Changing Role of the American Corporation* (Boston: Harvard Business School Press, 1999).
2 Frederick Reichheld and Thomas Teal, *The Loyalty Effect: The Hidden Force Behind Growth, Profits, and Lasting Value* (Boston: Harvard University Press, 1996).
3 Deb McCusker, Ilene Wolfman, "Loyalty in the Eyes of Employers and Employees," *Workforce*, November 1, 1998, p. 12.
4 "Alignment: The Last Frontier for Creating Competitive Advantage," results of Watson Wyatt Worldwide's 1997 Work USA study.
5 Mark A. Huselid, *The Impact of Human Resource Management Practices on Turnover, Productivity, and Corporate Financial Performance*, Academy of Management Journal, Vol. 38, No. 3, 1995, p. 638.
6 "The Towers Perrin Workplace Index," Towers Perrin, 1997.
7 Alignment, p. 2.
8 Peter F. Drucker, "What Businesses Can Learn from Non-Profits," *Harvard Business Review*, July-August 1989, pp. 88-93.
9 "The Towers Perrin Workplace Index," Towers Perrin, 1997, p. 5.
10 Alignment, p. 2.
11 Michael West and Malcolm Patterson, "Profitable Personnel," *People Management*, 8 January 1998, p. 28.
12 Jay Stuller, "The Renewal," *Chevron Now*, July 1998, p. 28.
13 Jay Stuller, "The Workforce Renewal Factor," *Strategy @ Work*, July 1999, pp. 17-20.
14 Alignment, p. 4.
15 Huselid, p. 640.
16 *Ibid.*
17 "The Human Capital Index: Linking Human Capital and Shareholder Value," Watson Wyatt Worldwide survey, 2000.
18 Robert S. Kaplan and David P. Norton, "The Balanced Scorecard—Measures That Drive Performance," *Harvard Business Review*, January-February 1998.
19 Anthony J. Rucci, Steven P. Kirn, and Richard T. Quinn, "The Employee-Customer-Profit Chain at Sears," *Harvard Business Review*, January-February 1998.
20 Reprinted from *Delivering Results: A New Mandate for Human Resource Professionals*, edited by Dave Ulrich (Boston: Harvard Business School Press, 1998).
21 v. N. Whitman, pp. 56-57.

chapter

Creating Alignment

After completing this chapter, you should be able to:

- Understand the nature of alignment and why it is important.
- Recognize essential human resource strategies for achieving line of sight to goals.
- Understand how individual behavior reinforces strategic goals.
- Translate changed behavior into cultural norms and create a "self-aligning culture."

Keeping the Main Thing, the Main Thing

Jim Barksdale, former CEO of Netscape (now a division of America Online) reminds us how straightforward alignment is. As he puts it: "The main thing is to keep the main thing, the main thing."[1] However, that seems a lot simpler than it actually is.

A friend of ours invested in the stock market during the 1980s. Not a financial sophisticate, she spent a long time ruminating about investing in the market and where to put her funds. She created a well-balanced portfolio and waited for her money to grow. Then, in October 1987, the stock market fell by more than 500 points.

Devastated, the investor wound up standing in line to sell her holdings at a significant loss. Her downfall? Her inability to stay focused on the goal of buying excellent stocks and maintaining a long-term perspective that would lead to gains. She ignored the basic principle of investing: buy low and sell high. She lost sight of her goal in the anxiety of the moment.

Companies suffer from the same lapses. Driven by short-term needs that are influenced by economic conditions, perceived competitors' advantages, and fads, management acts in ways that are inconsistent with the basic principles they announced to their stakeholders. In the early 1990s, Kmart pursued a strategy aimed at acquiring specialty retail stores. In its zeal to diversify, it lost focus on the business strategy that catapulted it to the top of the retailing world: discount retailing. Over a period of five years, Kmart fell from first to third place, slipping behind Wal-Mart and Target. Revenues fell to one-third of Wal-Mart's. Stores became shabby and understocked. And employees lacked direction while morale plummeted. In short, Kmart failed to keep the "main thing, the main thing."

The contrast between companies can be dramatic. Some years ago, FedEx (formerly Federal Express) hired Watson Wyatt to produce an orientation film. As part of the development process, we randomly interviewed employees at work. We examined every step of their procedure, including collecting, dispatching, and delivering overnight packages. Each individual discussed what he or she was doing, why it was important to do a good job, and how his or her work contributed to the company's overall success. Most memorable was the comment one employee made while on his way to deliver packages. "I need to get it there before 10 a.m. If I don't, UPS will." His sentiments were echoed throughout the organization, without exception. Ultimately, that's the definition of alignment.

Still, staying focused is not easy:

> . . . the greatest challenge that managers face today—keeping their people and organizations centered in the midst of change. There are two aspects to this challenge. The first is to get everyone headed in the same direction with a shared

purpose. The second is to integrate the resources and systems of the organization to achieve that purpose—what we call the main thing.[2]

In hindsight, it's easy to see how a company loses focus. The real trick is to identify an organization's defining purpose and the specific steps that can lead to success. Yet, it's also essential to understand that some visions, no matter how ingenious, can cause a company to founder. To say an organization is centered only begs the question "Centered on what?" To understand what makes companies successful requires a definition of the "main thing."

The "main thing" has been referred to as vision, mission, or purpose. As this chapter will illustrate, it is the crucial element in creating alignment. No matter what you call it, the "main thing" subsumes business strategy, core competencies, capacity, and culture. Successful organizations balance these elements as they grow and move toward a unified purpose.

Figure 3.1

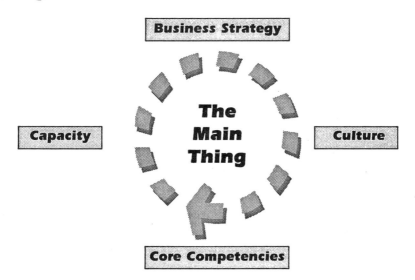

Business Strategy

Business strategy lies at the heart of action. On a most basic level, it rests on understanding opportunities in the marketplace and how to exploit them. A well conceived business strategy starts with a focus on the market and potential customers. This focus is the "vision." Then, an organization assesses which specific products and services its target market needs or wants. At this point, the firm organizes these processes to link the vision and the business strategy. It matches current staff against business needs. Finally, based on predetermined definitions of success, managers develop appropriate tools to measure goals against reality.

Of course, being good at what you do is different from what you do and why you do it. In the 1970s and 1980s, Japanese cars drove American cars off the road. The reason: Japanese automakers developed processes that permitted them to produce high-quality cars at a lower cost than American counterparts. Yet, as these Japanese companies discovered, such improvements don't automatically guarantee long-term financial success. While these Japanese firms enjoyed an advantage for a few years, today high quality is a given. What's more, strategic alliances and mergers have allowed competitors to leapfrog Japanese manufacturers. As widely respected business strategist Michael Porter notes, increasing operational effectiveness is not a substitute for having a strategy that makes a company unique in the marketplace.[3]

Capacity

As defined here, "capacity" is the measure of the resources necessary to produce goods or services. It represents both tangible capital (buildings, machinery, cash, etc.) and intangible capital (e.g., customer goodwill, workforce capabilities, employees, etc.). In his book on intellectual capital, Thomas Stewart identifies three categories: customer capital, structural capital, and human capital.

◆ **Structural capital** represents the collective knowledge of the organization—the stuff that does not go home at night. It belongs to the organization as a whole. It can be reproduced and shared. Much of what's included in the category of structural capital can be owned legally and includes technologies, inventions, data, publications, and processes that can be protected by patent, copyright, and other means. Structural capital also includes other elements that cannot be codified, such as strategy and culture. It includes organizational routines, systems, and procedures.[4]

◆ **Customer capital** is the value of an organization's client relationships. In other words, it is the likelihood that customers will keep doing business with the organization.[5]

◆ **Human capital** defines the ability of an organization to innovate through its people. The more an organization taps into this knowledge base to advance its business growth, the more its human capital is deployed. Repetitive, low-skill activity that offers little opportunity for individuals to use their knowledge or improve what they do typically falls outside the definition of human capital. Usually, these functions can be automated. Workers can be replaced because the work requires minimal talent and virtually no opportunity for contribution.[6]

Enterprise capacity can also be measured by financial wherewithal. Innovation requires investment in human, customer, and structural capital, and these usually (but not always) depend on an organization's ability to use its financial capital effectively. When you are steering a ship at sea, you must maintain sufficient speed to make the required maneuvers. This forward progress is called *way*. If there is no *way*, it does not matter if you turn the wheel; the ship will not respond. Financial capital plays a similar role in enhancing a company's ability to innovate.

Core Competencies

Core competencies represent the unique way a company organizes its work, develops its technologies, and delivers value. An organization must understand what's possible, given its collection of relevant skills and experience. For example, Sony's competency in the area of miniaturization enabled it to capture a large percentage of the consumer electronics business in the 1980s. Wal-Mart's unique approach to customer focus and pricing, and its unique logistical warehousing, represent core competencies.[7] Competencies determine how a company approaches a strategic problem and produces a product or service. It is difficult, although not impossible, to learn new competencies, but it is possible to acquire them.

A business that strays from its core knowledge and experience base is unlikely to succeed. Witness the horizontal conglomerates of the 1970s. These companies sought to develop managers who could oversee any of the company's diverse holdings and frequently rotated managers among business units. The problem with this approach is that it undervalues the unique competencies of each organization. What did the management team at Mobil, for example, understand about maximizing the competencies of Montgomery Ward?

Conversely, a company without a strategy—even one that maximizes its core competencies—risks over-adapting to its economic environment. When these companies lose their competitive edge in the marketplace, competencies become a less significant factor in business success, and organizations become vulnerable. For example, the Japanese automotive industry maximized its competency in quality management, continuous improvement, consensus management, and customer service, but minimized the need for a strategy. The industry focused on winning through better processes, not necessarily a better strategic vision. Process improvements can take a company only so far, particularly as competitors improve their own process. Competitors began to match their quality and customer service, and the Japanese manufacturers lacked a strategic framework that would have kept them one step ahead of the competition.[8]

Culture

Culture can be defined as a set of norms that characterize an organization and shape the behavior of individuals and groups within it. Norms, in turn, are expectations regarding which behaviors are appropriate and which are inappropriate.[9]

Each of us carries a different constellation of cultures—elements of national, ethnic, geographic, familial, and organizational cultures. Individual behavior is framed by cultural norms to produce generally predictable behaviors. In short, culture shapes behavior and influences the choices that an individual makes.

Corporations represent a subculture of separate norms, created at the start by those who shared a vision and a determined way of implementing that vision. In contrast with society at large, corporations, particularly those in the United States, can select employees who reinforce desired cultural norms and deselect those who act contrary to expected behaviors. In so doing, they can influence which norms are reinforced and which are extinguished. Over time, new leaders, different generational attitudes, and different business experiences shape behavior and, ultimately, culture. However, without firing everyone, elements of the old culture—passed on from seasoned employees to newer ones—will persist, often long after they have lost their relevance.

Culture bends, but does not break. It does not suddenly change; it evolves. It lends stability in times of chaos and resistance in times of change. The statement we at Watson Wyatt often hear clients say at the beginning of an assignment—"We need to change the culture"—really means "We need to change enough individual behaviors in order to change cultural norms." Culture is the residue of collective behaviors. Hence, getting people to change their behavior is where cultural change starts.

Business cultures filter action in different ways. Rob Goffee and Gareth Jones developed a typology of various corporate cultures. The framework is based on two elements: *solidarity* and *sociability*. Solidarity is the way the individuals within the organization share objectives and how effectively the group pursues them. Sociability is defined by sincerity and friendliness within the organization. In an organization that displays a high degree of solidarity, relationships are built around participation in common tasks and shared goals that will benefit everyone within the organization. Sociable organizations generally sustain themselves through face-to-face interactions with colleagues who share the same values and interests. This type of environment fosters teamwork, information sharing, and creativity.

Where culture hinders organizational change, the first focus should be on changing patterns of behavior that resist new organizational goals. Short of terminating entire workforces, companies in this situation need to streamline their reward structure. Socializing people to new ways of approaching problems is part of the solution. However, it is a slow and less efficient process by itself.

Organizational cultures exhibit both types of behaviors, but often one predominates over the other. Figure 3.2 illustrates the range of combinations.

Figure 3.2
Cultural Dimensions

		Low Solidarity	High Solidarity
Sociability	High	Networked "Getting around the hierarchy"	Communal "We're in this together"
	Low	Fragmented "What organization?"	Mercenary "We're all business"

Organizations that display both attributes—sociability and solidarity—are considered *communal* organizations. They are characteristic of small, fast-growing, entrepreneurial start-ups. In the early years, employees at Apple Computer not only shared the business mission at work, but also shared their lives outside of work.

At the other end of the spectrum are *fragmented* organizations, which display little sense of organizational membership or common understanding of organizational mission. Employees do not socialize outside of work. Frequently, members of such organizations identify more with a profession such as law or medicine rather than the identity of their specific organization. Leaders often feel isolated and ineffective, since consensus around business issues is often difficult to achieve. Not surprisingly, law firms, consulting firms, or similar professional firms typify fragmented environments. They're also found in manufacturing environments that rely on outsourcing of piecework.

Networked organizations are less characterized by their hierarchies than by informal paths used to navigate the environment. Whom you know is more important than following the "chain of command." Internal focus and office politics drive the organization's agenda often at the expense of customer or market demands. Unilever is an example of a networked organization where sociability is cultivated, but cross-company coordination and agreement on objectives has traditionally been hard to achieve.

Despite profound changes in the workplace, *mercenary* organizations still exist. Work and social life are clearly separate. Nike is known for its single-minded focus and its fierce competitiveness, but less for its internal camaraderie. Another company, Mastiff Wear, displays a sense of business urgency at the expense of building internal relationships. At Mastiff, employees work long hours and are expected to adhere to strict performance standards at all times. There the culture revolves around extensive internal competition and a relentless focus on achieving tasks that leaves little or no room for underachievers.[10]

These cultural dimensions both facilitate and limit business strategy. New messages and communications are filtered through existing cultural channels and norms. Understanding the structured organizational reaction to change is critical. It will dictate how messages need to be communicated, to whom and by whom. The converse is also true: trying to stretch a culture beyond its capabilities spells failure. Change can be brought about by overwhelming internal consensus and sponsorship, or by a business crisis that demands new ways of doing things. Either way, culture change is a formidable challenge.

Figure 3.3
The "Main Thing"

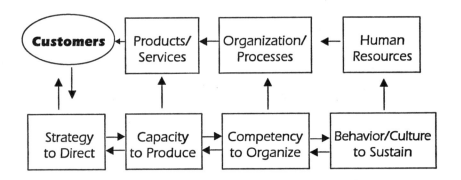

Establishing the "main thing" is the first step toward creating alignment. Statements of mission, purpose, philosophy, values, and strategy all must ratify some aspect of the main thing. These declarations must:[11]

- Provide a common and unifying concept to which every unit can contribute.

- Be clear and consistent with the organization's business goals, and actionable by every group and individual.

- Speak to each department, team, and individual in a way that establishes a direct link between their activities and operating norms and the success of the organization's strategy.

As shown in Figure 3.3, a successful strategic implementation links each of these factors together. Business strategies fail for any number of reasons, but failures generally occur because the connections between any of these elements break down. For example, a strategy that doesn't take into account what customers want and would be willing to pay for will not succeed. Likewise, a culture that resists efforts to organize around a given strategy is doomed.

Creating Alignment: Doing the "Right Thing"

Creating and communicating the "main thing" cannot alone create alignment. An excellent strategy that is poorly implemented is worse than a mediocre strategy that is well executed. Ultimately, people must not only know the "main thing," they must know how to do the "right thing" to create alignment. In this context, the right thing translates into activities that further corporate strategic goals and are consistent with capacity, competency, and culture.

Creating Alignment

Establishing a connection between corporate strategy and individual behavior creates alignment. As in the example of FedEx, each employee in an aligned organization understands how individual behavior and commitment contributes to overall corporate success. When business strategy changes or evolves, the human resource strategy must adapt to the new reality and help define employee behavior.

Developing human resource programs and policies, including a pay and benefits philosophy that supports HR strategy, is the next critical step toward creating line of sight. If done correctly (see Chapters **four** and **six**), these elements become primary drivers in reinforcing individual behavior, thus furthering HR and business strategies. Changing individual behavior eventually leads to changes in corporate culture.

Figure 3.4
Alignment: Creating Line of Sight Through Rewards

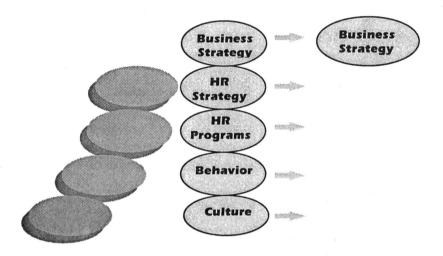

An aligned organization balances its strategy with its people's ability to comprehend and execute that strategy. Similarly, business processes need to support the delivery of goods and services to a company's employee. Labovitz and Rosansky divide alignment into two types: vertical and horizontal. Vertical alignment is the connection between a business strategy and the people who need to carry it forward. In this model, employees understand organizational goals and, most importantly, know what they need to do to help the organization achieve them.

Horizontal alignment refers to the relationship between employees in various functional areas and the processes created to deliver services and products to the market. It is important to understand what the customer wants, as well as how to deliver it. Ultimately, this leads to greater customer satisfaction.

Figure 3.5
The Alignment Paradigm

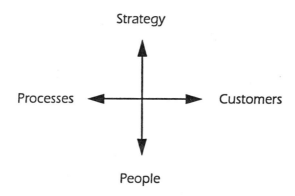

Alignment occurs when these elements are balanced. Breakdowns occur when people work too hard to satisfy customer needs that no longer exist, when there is no clear strategy, and when the strategy is not effectively deployed. As demonstrated in Figure 3.5, creating alignment requires establishing line-of-sight goals from people to strategy and from process to customer satisfaction. However, to establish the connection, businesses must understand what it takes to satisfy customers. They should ask:

◆ Are we selling the kinds of goods and/or services the market demands?

◆ Is our pricing competitive?

◆ Is our customer experience pleasant and distinctive?

◆ Can our business processes deliver the product for a cost that will ensure a profit?

◆ Are we efficiently organized?

◆ Do we have the right staff?

Connecting people to strategy likewise requires an understanding of what it takes to align employee behaviors with business goals:

◆ Do employees thoroughly understand the strategy?

◆ Is the strategy within the competency and capability of the organization? If not, how do we acquire those competencies and capabilities? If yes, how do we retain those skills critical to the achievement of the corporate mission?

◆ Do employees understand specifically how their behaviors help to further the strategy?

◆ Is our performance development process built around the achievement of these goals?

◆ Do we effectively reward the achievement of strategic goals?

Addressing the issues raised by these questions establishes a line of sight between processes and customers. It also reinforces alignment between people and strategy.

Human Resources' Role in Creating Alignment

Chapter **two** examined the role of human resources in strategic hiring, wiring, and retiring. To be successful, a human resources strategy must integrate traditional personnel activities with more progressive strategic roles. The human resources department is charged with four important management responsibilities:[12]

1. Strategic human resources

2. Transformation and change

3. Company infrastructure

4. Employee contribution

To be effective, each of these areas must be linked functionally, and must fit into an HR management strategy that contributes to the organization's success. Thus, managing strategy infrastructure, organizational change, and employee needs must be pointed toward accomplishing the specific organizational trends of hiring, wiring, and retiring.

The activities in each one of these functional areas must answer these questions:

◆ *Hiring*. How does it help us acquire the right employees?

◆ *Wiring*. How does it help us retain valued employees? How does it help us engage employees in the corporate mission?

◆ *Retiring*. How do we move people through the workforce? As business strategies change, how do we transition employees to other activities within the company or, if necessary, to employment outside the company or to retirement?

1. *Managing Strategic Human Resources.* Aligning human resources with business strategy and helping to execute that strategy is a pivotal role of the human resources function. Creating a human resources strategy that supports business goals elevates the human resource function from administrator to strategic business partner. At a minimum, the human resource strategy must:

◆ Set forth a corporate mission statement and philosophy that establishes the ground rules for managing human capital.

◆ Identify the functional requirements involving human capital, which support and/or advance the business strategy.

- ◆ Assess organizational capacity and competence in functions critical to the success of the business strategy. Develop plans to address gaps in these areas.

- ◆ Establish programs such as compensation systems, training and development programs, recruitment activities, retention strategies, and other human resource programs that reward positive behaviors.

2. *Managing transformation and change.* Human resources professionals function as shock troops during change initiatives. They create a framework for change by communicating the new strategic mission and/or integrating new cultures and aligning them with the business strategy. As change agents, HR professionals lead reorganization efforts by identifying issues, helping to establish action plans, solving problems, and overseeing implementation of these activities. All this is magnified during the integration of cultures during a merger, with cultural integration being added to the list of change management activities.

3. *Managing company infrastructure.* It is one of the sad truths of corporate life that the successful management of a firm's infrastructure is often not as widely recognized as being critical to the mission of hiring, wiring, and retiring. This is because efficient administration is expected. It is only when the opposite occurs that we notice the havoc created. For example, payroll managers rarely receive praise for ensuring that payroll checks are correct. However, mistakes generate anger and reprimand because employees become irritated. If these mistakes aren't addressed, wholesale disaffection occurs. Managers of infrastructure are charged with ensuring that administrative jobs are complete, which forces them to continually evaluate and reengineer these processes to ensure efficient operation. In short, failure to deliver in this area can destroy alignment and torpedo the corporate mission.

4. *Managing employee contribution.* When employees make their individual contributions to the business in a way that meets the corporate goals, alignment takes place. Articulating and communicating a clear human resources strategy while successfully managing infrastructure, transformation, and change are important elements in creating employee engagement. However, success in these arenas does not necessarily lead to employee commitment. Alignment with the business strategy can only be achieved when:[13]

◆ The business strategy is clearly articulated and communicated.

◆ The human resource strategy supports the business strategy by establishing programs, plans, and policies that reinforce the business strategy.

◆ Employees understand how their activities contribute to the furtherance of corporate goals, i.e., by establishing a line of sight to the business strategy.

◆ Performance criteria reinforce these line-of-sight activities.

◆ Achievement of these performance criteria determines rewards.

Each of these four functional roles influences the individual behaviors that will cause a strategy to succeed or fail. Getting people to do the right thing requires an understanding of how each business and staff function fits into the overall business strategy. One of the most common problems occurs when the connection to the business model is too fuzzy. For a line of sight to exist between the organization's strategic goals and an individual's contribution, each employee needs to comprehend the mission of his own business unit and how it contributes to the success of the company. Developing individual mission statements for each major business unit and corporate function is a start. Building business processes around the strategic mission continually reminds employees of their expected behavior.

case study

Integrating Business Strategy with Employee Behavior: Toyota's Approach

A nagging problem affecting organizational success is balancing cross-functional integration and functional expertise. In the automobile industry, this translated into the need to integrate product design and manufacturing-process design with outside departments, such as marketing, purchasing, and finance. In an attempt to address the challenge, organizations turned to everything from product development tools to assigning individuals to temporary project teams or organizing around product lines.

While these methods improved product development results, they also created their own set of headaches: loss of expertise because people spent less time in their professional functions; loss of standardization due to the independence of project teams; and conflicting directives as team members were torn between commands from their functional leaders and the demands of their project team leaders. Meanwhile, Toyota, one of the world's leading automobile manufacturers, attacked the issue of vehicle development in a different way. Toyota relied on highly formalized rules and standards. While cross-functional teams are used, their interaction is limited.

The Toyota process recognizes that workers have expertise in functional areas and the organization assigns them to work on projects based on specific needs of project leaders. In a sense, this represents a contingent labor pool within the company. In order for this work model to succeed and not become mired in time-consuming meetings, the company has enacted specific policies surrounding the way employees communicate.

One key practice is requiring workers to resolve issues in writing. First, a brief, standardized report is generated. It diagnoses a problem and provides key information along with recommendations. The report is distributed to project members. A short meeting or telephone call usually accompanies the report to emphasize a point or highlight key information. The expectation is that people will read the report and offer comments.

Mentoring supervisors, whose role is to build deep functional expertise, teach newer engineers how to handle report writing and reading efficiently. After one or two iterations, most issues are resolved. Any continued disagreements are resolved at a meeting, where participants discuss key issues and come to an understanding.

Design project leaders integrate the work of people from diverse specialties. These individuals—Chief Engineers in Toyota's parlance—oversee long-term planning across projects. They maintain full responsibility for a single vehicle program, but have no direct authority over the functional areas. Instead, a chief engineer's extensive technical expertise is expected to provide leadership over the functional engineers. Unresolved issues between the chief engineer and functional engineers are elevated to a higher level and resolved by general managers of the functional areas. In short, a chief engineer is less a manager in the traditional sense and more a lead designer for a given project.

Toyota also has a unique approach to skills development. Unlike most companies, Toyota rotates most of its engineers within only one function. Rotations generally occur for more than one product cycle so that engineers can see the results of their work. For example, body engineers will work on different auto-body subsystems. This tends to standardize each function, encourages expertise, and helps in coordinating tasks within the functional area. As senior engineers gain knowledge, they are rotated through various parts of the organization. This is the opposite of traditional American human resources practice, which slots senior personnel into management positions within their own discipline. Rotations increase communication between functions and help to expand networks of coordination.

By using this process, which provides a longer period of time for skill development, Toyota keeps the time invested in coordinating production to a minimum. In other car companies, these work processes specify in detail the content of each method. Such practice ensures consistent work process within a predictable time. By relying on the intense socialization of engineers through on-the-job training, Toyota keeps standardized work plans to a minimum. This permits the flexibility to respond to the unique challenges of each project. At the same time, standard work procedures are maintained by the people who use them and not by a centralized staff with less knowledge of specific work processes.[14]

Toyota's approach to product development may not be appropriate for every company. Furthermore, it may not be the best way to organize production. Yet as we examine the company's approach closely, the skeleton of an outlined process emerges. Elements of business strategy, HR strategy and programs, expected behavior, and finally a predictable culture are all there.

The following chart illustrates the interconnection of Toyota's business strategy with HR strategy, which in turn affects behavior.

Figure 3.6
Connecting to Business Strategy: New Product Development at Toyota

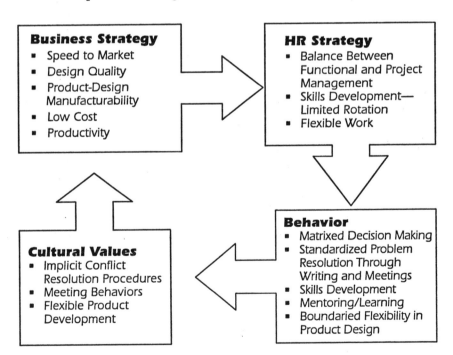

Business Strategy
- Speed to Market
- Design Quality
- Product-Design Manufacturability
- Low Cost
- Productivity

HR Strategy
- Balance Between Functional and Project Management
- Skills Development—Limited Rotation
- Flexible Work

Cultural Values
- Implicit Conflict Resolution Procedures
- Meeting Behaviors
- Flexible Product Development

Behavior
- Matrixed Decision Making
- Standardized Problem Resolution Through Writing and Meetings
- Skills Development
- Mentoring/Learning
- Boundaried Flexibility in Product Design

Established norms, resulting from consistently reinforced behaviors, formed part of Toyota's corporate culture. Finally, the norms and values associated with the development process reinforce the business strategy as well as individual behaviors.

Emphasizing the main thing—even at the project level—reinforces alignment. Fluor Daniel is one of the world's largest engineering and construction firms. It established an alignment process that connects the clients, vendors, and workers. The process begins when employees share an understanding of the project's purpose throughout the value chain. After this, the firm assigns seven deliverables to ensure that workers meet overall objectives:[15]

1. Shared Project Values: Trust innovation flexibility, and open communications.

2. A Purpose Statement: An outline of expected results.

3. Key Result Areas: Objectives such as safety, cost-effectiveness, timely performance, and quality.

4. Measurement: Mechanisms to measure Key Result Areas.

5. Critical Activities: The actions necessary to achieve Key Results Areas.

6. Role Clarification: Clearly stated team roles and responsibilities.

7. Path Forward: Identification of action teams and measurement strategies.

This type of tool, which not only measures the effectiveness of the project but forces participants to restate corporate values and define the project purpose, reinforces business strategy and corporate culture. However, rules by themselves do not create alignment.

It's whether individuals follow the rules. And getting them to do that consistently requires continual reinforcement of company strategy.

Staying Aligned:
Keeping the Main Thing, the Main Thing

Business realities constantly change. Sometimes the change is dramatic, such as when a new invention revolutionizes an old routine. Inventions like the telegraph, the electric light, the internal combustion engine, the personal computer, and the Internet are examples of technologies that opened new doors for business. That combined with economic conditions related to the business cycle, force established businesses to tack one way or the other. Countless other factors, ranging from societal attitudes to the state of the competitive landscape, force incremental changes in business process. Some of these are short-term blips; others foretell a sea of change in the way we do business.

In response, organizations must constantly tweak and reexamine business strategies. Years ago, we knew a man whose job it was to manage the five-year plan at a large corporation. His task was not just to develop the plan and wait around for five years to see how it turned out. Instead, he monitored projections against reality and each year came up with a new five-year plan that outlined the corporate strategy. The point is that business strategy must constantly change—sometimes a little, sometimes a lot—to keep up with an evolving market.

Achieving success with any given business strategy requires that an organization mold individual behaviors. Above all else, that means telling employees how they will be measured and then measuring them. As we discussed in Chapter **two**, a balanced scorecard can effectively measure and manage employee and customer attitudes. When an effective system is introduced, and connected to performance and rewards, performance and productivity can soar. Suddenly, all systems are in place to reinforce individual behaviors. We have often told clients: "If you want it, measure it. If you need it, pay for it." Translating this phrase to reality requires four specific actions. You must:

◆ Translate goals into specific activities and behaviors.

◆ Communicate organizational goals and expectations.

◆ Measure performance against those expectations.

◆ Reward individuals based on measurement.

Figure 3.7
Keeping the Main Thing, the Main Thing

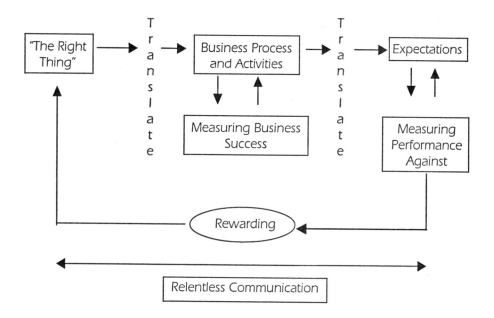

By understanding the necessary capabilities, competencies, and cultural values that must be translated into activities and behaviors critical to the success of a business, you can take a giant step toward success. Yet, these required behaviors also must be linked to specific performance expectations. Managers must communicate to employees at the beginning of the performance period—not the end—the set of expectations. At the same time, rewards must center on the attainment of these expectations.

This does not mean that an organization should exclude individual growth opportunities from the process. To the contrary, both managers and employees need to identify such opportunities because they advance the overall mission of a company by beefing up an organization's competencies and capabilities.

In the end, success rests as much on the activities of translating, communicating, and rewarding as it does on the design of individual business processes and performance management programs. Translating strategy, capabilities, competencies, and culture into sustainable business processes requires a clear understanding of what can be done and how it can be accomplished. Toyota, for instance, developed appropriate processes around the corporate need for an efficient, cross-functional design process.

Of course, someone still had to establish processes to get the job done. In some instances, these were formal procedures. But in other cases they were informal—revolving around cultural norms and attitudes. Similarly, it's possible to establish expectations as the performance yardstick. This requires translating processes into specific goals and clearly communicating what behaviors make business processes succeed. Without targeted, convincing, and frequent communications, expectations slowly drift away from the corporate mission. Rewarding the achievement of expected goals completes the loop and reinforces the "main thing."

The challenge in creating alignment comes down to "saying what you mean, doing what you say, and rewarding what was done." This "virtuous circle" sustains business strategy and keeps the company aligned with its preordained future.

Notes

[1] George Labovitz and Victor Rosansky, *The Power of Alignment: How Great Companies Stay Centered and Accomplish Extraordinary Things* (New York: John Wiley & Sons, Inc., 1997).

[2] George Labovitz and Victor Rosansky, p. 3.

[3] M. Porter, "What Is Strategy," Reprinted in *Delivering Results*, Edited by David Ulrich (Boston: Harvard Business Review Press, 1998), p. 99.

[4] Thomas Stewart, *Intellectual Capital: How the Knowledge Economy is Creating New Challenges for Corporations & New Opportunities for the People Who Work for Them* (New York: Doubleday, 1997), p. 109.

[5] Thomas Stewart, p. 77.

[6] Thomas Stewart, pp. 86-87.

[7] C.P. Prahalad and Gary Hamel, "The Core Competence of the Corporation," Reprinted in *Delivering Results*, Edited by David Ulrich (Boston: Harvard Business Review Press, 1998), p. 49.

[8] M. Porter, p. 97.

[9] Elizabeth F. Cabrera, "An Expert HR System for Aligning Organizational Culture and Strategy," *Human Resource Planning*, Volume 22.1, 1999.

[10] Rob Goffee and Gareth Jones, "What holds the Modern Company Together," *Harvard Business Review*, November-December 1996, p. 140.

[11] George Labovite and Victor Rosansky, p. 44.

[12] David Ulrich, *Human Resource Champions: The Next Agenda for Adding Value and Delivering Results* (Boston: Harvard Business School Publishing, 1996).

[13] David Ulrich, *Human Resource Champions*, pp. 24-25.

[14] Durward K. Sobek, II, Jeffrey K. Liker, Alan C. Ward, "Another Look at How Toyota Integrates Product Development," *Harvard Business Review*, July-August 1998, p. 36.

[15] George Labovitz and Victor Rosansky, p. 136.

chapter

A Compelling Human Resources Strategy

After completing this chapter, you should be able to:

- ◆ Understand the "new employment contract" and the career stage continuum.
- ◆ Identify career stage differences and how these differences affect employee motivation.
- ◆ Design a human resource strategy.

The New Employee-Employer Contract

In today's workplace, the promise of loyalty in exchange for job security no longer exists. The rules have all changed. In the new corporate pact, there are no long-term commitments and there is no shared responsibility. Today, employees are loyal to the company only as long as it benefits them personally. The idea of *job security* is replaced by *career security*. To attract the best and brightest individuals, smart management must provide workers with skill-enhancing career opportunities, help in managing their own careers, and benefits that they can take with them when they leave. As Helen Axel, senior research fellow at The Conference Board, puts it:

> Under the new employment compact, companies are increasingly making greater demands on employees, but at the same time, offer far less than a secure, lifelong place to work. Skills and performance are replacing dedication and loyalty as conditions for continued employment. However, employees have clear expectations about their employers, and in an era when motivation, commitment, and talent are in short supply, organizations are beginning to be more responsive to employee needs.[1]

According to the Conference Board, 67 percent of companies surveyed believe that the contract has vanished or is now being redefined. Most interestingly, 61 percent of surveyed companies believe employees are willing partners in the current employment relationship. These employees do not expect the same level of job security and protection as did their predecessors in the 1980s. They understand the need to take responsibility for their own skills and education—that career security is replacing job security.

Self-service has become a new buzzword in corporate America. Understanding the pivotal position that HR professionals play in this compact, companies have begun to devise self-directed training and development opportunities for employees as well as provide them the opportunity to make their own choices about benefits. Corporate Intranets are now instrumental in validating this model. They provide the tools for workers to update and change their employment data, let them handle their own investments through a 401(k) plan, and keep them informed about policies, procedures, and opportunities—including job openings and career opportunities within the company.

Make no mistake, the U.S. work environment is a completely different landscape than ten, even five years ago. It is one that our parents and grandparents would hardly recognize. Employee and employer expectations have evolved. Both parties have become accustomed to the notion that employment is "at will" and can be terminated based on changed personal or business circumstances.

In addition, employees have become more committed to personal growth. As a result, today the employment relationship is more a "strategic partnership" in which both sides pledge mutual commitment. When the commitment is no longer there, the relationship ends. Figure 4.1 illustrates this evolution.

Figure 4.1
The New Employee-Employer Contract

	Old World "Keep your nose clean and you have a job for life"	Restructured "Work smarter not harder"	The New Contract "Balanced reciprocity"
If You	Are loyal Work hard Do as you're told	Stay Do your job plus someone else's Do as you're told	Develop skills that we need Apply them in ways that help the company succeed Behave consistently with our new values
We Will	Provide a secure job Award steady pay increases Provide financial security	Provide a job (if we can) Make gestures that we care Provide the same pay	Provide challenging work Support your development Reward your contribution Treat you like an adult

This landscape is continuing to change rapidly. The economic, political, and sociological realities of the new millennium are complex. Charting a course through these waters is incredibly difficult. Even the most progressive companies are finding their human resource policies and practices stretched and reshaped with remarkable frequency.

What Makes a Workplace Click

It is not difficult to spot a compelling place to work. Once you step through the front door and wander along the desks or cubicles, you sense that excitement and purpose fill the air. Employees are engaged in their work and they like being there. When you come into contact with these people—on the phone, through e-mail, or in person—you can sense the company's momentum. Instead of getting stuck on problems and looking for reasons not to move forward, the organization has a collective sense that it can achieve desired results and beat the competition.

The workforce has a sense of confidence, not arrogance. It respects competitors, and it understands the dynamics of the industry and the challenges of today's business climate. Yet, employees know that they are playing a role in something meaningful and important. They are building a vision of the future, and feel they are part of the process rather than cogs in a giant wheel. Their ideas, thoughts, opinions, and knowledge count for something. The organization acknowledges their contribution.

At these companies, empowerment is not a tired, worn phrase. Instead, it is an active belief system that helps create a line of sight so that workers can see the direct results of their contributions. Moreover, workplace flexibility and virtual work are not HR mantras; they are tied to productivity and results. Performance management thrives (Chapter **seven** will cover this topic in greater detail), and the overall culture is one where employees feel there is some balance between work and life. On the compensation front, targeted, well-conceived strategies help retain the best workers and reward those who make the greatest contribution.

How are these workplaces created? What magic do chief executive officers and other senior executives use to build a culture that values the individual and the group? How does HR invoke the policies and practices to create such a place? What is in it for shareholders? These are complex questions that cannot be solved by applying a set of basic principles. A far more comprehensive and global view is necessary.

On the human side, the answers center on recognizing the demographics of the workforce, understanding how career stages and generational differences affect attitudes and perceptions, and addressing the needs of today's workers. On the practical side, it is about creating meaningful work, fostering an environment that stimulates and rewards people appropriately, and giving a workforce the tools to develop a line of sight. When all of these pieces converge, it is possible to generate synergy and momentum that can boost performance, employee satisfaction, and shareholder value.

People Strategy and Shareholder Value

The cumulative and consistent evidence is that having a smart human capital strategy leads to superior financial results. A 2000 survey of over 550 U.S. employers, conducted by Watson Wyatt Worldwide, found that while fewer than 14 percent of companies surveyed view their people strategy as a source of competitive advantage, those that do have nearly twice the shareholder return of companies that do not.[2] This same survey indicates that for companies whose employees believe that true pay for performance is practiced, average total shareholder returns during the period from 1996 to 1998 were 112 percent, compared with 80 percent for companies whose employees believe it is not practiced. Similarly, companies whose employees are highly committed also outperform other companies by a significant margin.

Figure 4.2
Effect of Employee Commitment
on Shareholder Return

Employee Commitment	Average Total Return to Shareholders 1996-1998
Low employee commitment	76%
Medium employee commitment	90%
High employee commitment	112%

Understanding the Attributes of the "New Company"

The evolution from a command and control culture to an organization based on teams and knowledge sharing has not happened by accident. Information technology—e-mail, workflow over internal networks and the Web—has inexorably changed the possibilities and capabilities. It has allowed work to be performed across departments and geographical boundaries. It has made collaboration a necessity and let companies reengineer work and processes to slash administrative overhead, cut costs, and accomplish more with less.

Indeed, technology is driving enormous change. Today's systems effectively topple the vertical corporate structure of the past, which supported hierarchical decision making and knowledge hoarding. In today's world, managers must facilitate knowledge sharing and work as coaches to inspire and develop team capabilities. In the emerging Information Age economy, anything less is suicide.

The new company has the following characteristics:

◆ **Flatter**. Information technology and the reengineering of processes have changed the way organizations collect, manage, and exchange data. It has pushed decision making to the line and eliminated the need for many managers. Leaders play a very different role: they coach and facilitate and inspire, rather than make everyday decisions.

Work smarter, not harder really means something in today's environment. We have mowed down the redundancies and crumpled the inefficiencies. However, in making this change, we also have lost some of the corporate handholds—experienced managers who can mentor employees. It is not unusual for someone to say, "I need a mentor." That is code for, "Do I have anyone watching out for me?" Although the new organization might embrace a more horizontal structure, the needs of workers have not gone away. Ultimately, it is up to human resources departments to recognize and address this issue.

♦ **Virtual.** Today, anyone can work anywhere. Modems, faxes, e-mail, Web connectivity, and mobile phones shatter the walls of the traditional office. Knowledge workers can telecommute or operate entirely out of a home office or on the road. Workers now make the decision about where they work based partly on lifestyle issues, and companies cannot ignore this trend. Organizations are also driven by economics. The high cost of office space makes virtual workplaces a more enticing proposition.

Yet employees are not the whole story when it comes to a virtual workforce. The modern enterprise increasingly relies on independent contractors to fill roles and provide specialized expertise. It does not matter whether the need is for a programmer—who just happens to be located in India and is available at a lower cost—or a writer to create a brochure on a moment's notice. Connectivity makes it possible, and facilitates around-the-clock work.

Of course, engaging a workforce scattered across the globe is not painless, especially when the workforce comprises both employees and non-employees. Maintaining a cohesive culture, communicating goals and expectations, and forging a shared vision that meshes with the organization's overall business objectives requires a highly focused approach. HR must understand this emerging labor model and use it effectively in order to compete effectively. It must differentiate its core constituency from those who ratchet up value but are not integral to the culture.

♦ **Greater consolidation.** Mergers and acquisitions have become a routine part of the business landscape over the last decade. However, the effect they have on a workforce is anything but routine. Harvard University's Michael Porter, in a landmark May 1987 *Harvard Business Review* article, argued persuasively that most would-be synergies from mergers are never realized. Gemini Consulting has found that 50 percent of all merged companies fail to maintain their book value two years after the merger. In many instances, it is more about cultural incompatibilities and failings than a lack of synergy between business lines.

Indeed, whether an organization is buttoned-down and bottom-line oriented or laid back and spontaneous makes a huge difference. When organizations merge, one of the biggest potential problems is losing the people who have contributed most to each organization's success. Another is seeing employees become disengaged and unmotivated. They might worry about how their job is going to change or whether the project they have spent the last six months working on is going to be axed. Regardless of the exact reason, it is crucial to address the human factor.

◆ **Engages in strategic and economic alliances.** Corporate alliances have gone mainstream, filtering through almost every industry and every type of company. In an era of intense global competition, it might seem a bit ironic that companies are collaborating like never before. In fact, collaboration is increasingly viewed as a ticket to greater performance and profits. According to John R. Harbison, a vice president for Booz Allen & Hamilton and author of *Smart Alliances: A Practical Guide to Repeatable Success* (Jossey-Bass, 1998), a well designed partnership can offer a 50 percent higher return on investment than a firm's base business. "It's an opportunity to pursue a business objective with only an incremental investment," he explains.

Unfortunately, a few potential snags exist. According to a study conducted by Alliance Management International Ltd., a Cleveland, Ohio consulting firm specializing in strategic alliances, more than 50 percent of partnerships fail, even when there are clear-cut advantages to working together. Too often, partnerships are poorly managed, cultures do not mesh, and participants have unrealistic expectations. As a result, it is essential to understand how alliances affect a workforce and take a proactive approach to defining an organization's strategy.

◆ **Market driven.** The reality of today's marketplace is sobering. Intense pricing pressure and competition is pushing companies to constantly move faster and produce products more cheaply. Organizations are looking for ways to reduce inventory, build a more efficient supply chain, and improve internal processes to get products to market more quickly and effectively. While technology might be the enabler, people develop ideas, refine concepts, design products, and provide customer service and technical support. Without the right set of attitudes, beliefs, and goals as part of a culture, an organization is at a huge disadvantage.

◆ **Global.** Today, it is possible to manufacture almost anywhere, or provide a service—such as technical support—without regard to geography. Computers have radically changed the way companies develop products and provide services. Add to all this growing global competition, and it is clear that the rules that guided companies in decades past no longer exist. Organizations now look for pockets of labor wherever they exist. That might mean moving a manufacturing operation to Singapore, outsourcing it to Brazil, or finding foreign labor to bring into a country.

It also means managing human resources data across countries and political systems. As the need for competency management grows, so too does the need for decision support systems, business intelligence to identify gaps and opportunities in dealing with human capital, the reliance on technology, and solid management practices. Again, linking disparate values and attitudes is essential. Without a cohesive view and supportive business culture, success is an uphill battle.

Identifying and Acknowledging the Primary Stakeholders

Stakeholders, whose needs and demands must constantly be balanced, pull today's enterprise in different directions. Each of these groups defines what actions and reactions take place, as well as how human resources and other departments forge policies, procedures, and strategies. It is impossible to implement an effective strategy without taking into account how each of these groups would be affected.

Employees: We have discussed today's workers at great length, suggesting that their outlook on employment has changed. This problem is exacerbated by the realities of today's demographics and the dramatic shortfall in the number of new entrants into the workforce. In short, it's a seller's market for labor, which will continue for some time.

As a result, organizations dependent on knowledge workers are much more dependent on catering to the needs of the new employee. We've seen companies add such benefits as child/elder care, fitness clubs or memberships, auto loan subsidies, concierge services, legal services, travel discounts, and financial planning to attract and retain a talented workforce. Companies more than ever must listen to what employees are saying or face the prospect of high turnover and a disaffected workforce. It goes almost without saying that human resource policies also have to be rational, flexible, and fair, and communicated and administered in a fashion that promotes these attributes.

Administrators: This constituency is perhaps the most ignored and abused of all. Companies can only deliver what its property, plant, and processes can handle. In the human resources area, it used to be that we designed plans and only later considered how they would be administered. Today, the expense of building complicated administrative systems to support plans or programs that are overly complicated has forced many organizations to reconsider what it is doing and why. Similarly, Byzantine or archaic accounting or financial systems that don't support corporate needs can turn a great strategic leap into a hobbled baby step. Infrastructure and administrative concerns and capabilities must be balanced with other corporate activities.

Financial: No company can operate without monetary investments. Yet, the nature of the funding—private or public, stock or loans—can greatly affect the way a company does business. Financial stakeholders—whether holding equity or debt—place demands on companies for investment returns and/or capital appreciation. The reaction of the financial community to a whole range of human resource practices and initiatives is today a critical consideration. How much executives are paid, takeover defenses that are incorporated into employee retirement plans, and organizational headcount are some areas that can, and do, affect the return on investment.

Financial stakeholders are not all on the outside of an organization. They are represented internally by the financial and accounting personnel with whom every organization is blessed. They too have an important say in not only what gets done, but how it gets done.

Customers: The good will a company possesses with its customers will only continue if the company listens and values what they have to say. Product pricing, convenience, quality, service, positive buying experience, and technical support are some of the tools at an organization's disposal that can promote customer loyalty. A crowded department store after Christmas in which customers are lined up, waiting to return purchases, while the harried clerk keys each item into the corporate inventory system is listening more to its financial and infrastructure stakeholders than to its customers.

Using the New Employee-Employer Contract as a Competitive Advantage

It is a new era. The mantra of the 1980s, "lean and mean," has been replaced with a different and more sensible mindset: *How can we, as an employer, recognize what people need and want to stay fully engaged in work? How can we as a company create an environment that benefits everyone?* Forging this new contract requires HR to understand that *loyalty* and *commitment* take on a far different meaning today than in generations past. Becoming an employer of choice is not just a good idea, it is essential.

Talk to people who work at Southwest Airlines or PeopleSoft. Or have a conversation with someone at Hewlett Packard or Merck. When *Fortune* magazine published its 1999 list, "The 100 Best Companies to Work for in America," they came out on top. They did not achieve this status by accident. They understand the new relationship, and they build their organizations to give employees an exciting and rewarding place to work. Almost every company that makes the *Fortune* list invests significantly in employee education and tuition reimbursement. They provide excellent "soft benefits," such as on-site haircuts and breakfasts, gym memberships, and inexpensive or free child care. They invariably give their employees autonomy to make decisions and solve problems.

As one consultant in the *Fortune* article explained:

> There are plenty of very good places to work. But the best organizations are taking a differentiation tack, much as a brand would do in a consumer market. The message has to be, "We stand for something that others don't. We're special. We're relevant."[3]

Companies like Microsoft and Xerox have figured this out. They have learned how to translate human capital into an enormous source of wealth. In 1996, Microsoft's market capitalization topped $85 billion, but its physical assets were worth only $1 billion. That means that by subtracting the physical assets from the market capitalization, the value of human contribution was $84 billion—or more than 98 percent. The same year, Xerox sported a 93 percent human contribution.

That is a far different scenario than an Industrial Age economy, which put a premium on physical capital, often at double the rate of today's Information Age. Increasingly, buildings, machinery, raw materials, and transportation pale in significance to brainpower, intellectual property, and data. Harnessing human capital—employees' knowledge, skills, experience, capabilities, and personal relationships—is at the center of this universe. That helps an organization meet the needs of its customers and shareholders, and it creates greater wealth for all.

The New Deal: Strategic Partnerships and Balanced Reciprocity

Effective HR strategy balances the business needs of the company's shareholders and customers with employee needs. It articulates the "value proposition." Simply stated, the "value proposition" is the *deal: what the employee gets for services that add value.*

Figure 4.3
Balanced Reciprocity

The business needs to ⟶ Attract, retain, and motivate
build capability and the most competent employees
achieve results:

Skills and competencies that
lead to superior performance

What's in it ⟶ A sustainable career:
for employees? Challenging work
Developmental opportunities
Competitive rewards

Articulating the Deal: HR Strategy

Employees, whether knowledge workers or parts assemblers, come to the workplace with a variety of expectations, attitudes, and capabilities. Based on personal experiences, work history, and personality, each worker presents a tremendous opportunity for the organization. Nevertheless, managing workers as a group opens a potential Pandora's box. Developing an overall human resources strategy can prove vexing. *What do workers want at different career stages? What motivates the typical entry-level or mid-career employee? How about established professionals? Which groups are more expensive?* Maybe most importantly, *Do workers' needs and expectations dovetail or clash with the organization's goals?*

Who are these employees? They are diverse top performers who are a company's stars: Generation X employees with technical skills, baby boomers looking for stability and the opportunity to save for retirement, and other employees that cross many of these different boundaries.

Finding the Right HR Strategy

A fact most companies have not dealt with yet is that different employees require different deals. If we had to characterize this shift in today's parlance, it would be reflected in the move from one-size-fits-all to "me.com." Research tells us that employees, whatever their skill level or value to the organization, want a more flexible deal with their employer. They want an HR package that is more customized to their needs. To be most effective, HR strategy must consider the work to be accomplished and the needs of organizational constituents, and identify the expected contributions of each. It must link the business plan with organizational roles, functional job duties, valued behaviors, and applied competencies important for business success. The following questions must be considered.

- ◆ How many employees (and at what career/capability level) does the business need to meet business objectives?

- ◆ Given the career/capability levels identified, what is the performance expectation and value proposition of employment? What commitment can be anticipated?

◆ What should the employee expect in terms of the intensity of the relationship? What should the organization expect?

The following chart organizes career/capability stages into four categories. The important point is that all organizations need all categories, only in different combinations and strengths. The task for an organization is to identify the right mix and then use it as a framework for considering HR designs and programs that create engagement, communication, education, and reinforcement.

Figure 4.4
Balancing the Deal

Career Stage	Investment → Entrant	Intellectual Capital → Contributor	Asset Producer	Expert
Value Proposition	Acquiring skills and competencies	Building personal capability and skills Performs tasks under the direction of others	Established reputation for productivity, competence, and sound judgment Demonstrates job mastery and manages details of work effectively Is a mentor	Creates proprietary intellectual property Solves the most complex and critical problems Recognized internally and externally as a "guru" Is a role model
Performance Expectation	Low competence and productivity	Moderate competence and productivity	High competence and productivity	Unique talent and competence Highly productive and innovative
Commitment	High	Variable	Moderate	High
Direction and Support	High	High direction and variable support Inspiration of leaders	Low direction and variable support Confidence in leaders	No direction High support Assumes leadership roles Confidence in business strategy

The Entrant

When it comes to identifying the right balance, entry-level workers are the most straightforward group. Their training, orientation, and need for direction and support is a cost of doing business. However, this group is the future of the enterprise and when effectively selected, a worthwhile investment. It is our experience that there is a spectrum of approaches in dealing with the new entrant—at one extreme the Guppy Approach, and at the other, the Baby Bird school of development.

Guppy Approach. The Guppy Approach brings in as many new entrants as possible. This strategy often corresponds to the labor intensity of the work itself. The idea is that through churn we meet our productivity needs, hold down our labor costs, and from time to time find "keepers" that we can promote. Day-to-day turnover is expected and taken in stride. From the employee perspective, this is a wonderful opportunity to gain experience, skills, and career momentum.

Baby Bird Approach. At the opposite end of the spectrum is the baby bird school of development. This strategy often corresponds to the need of the organization for a unique foundation of competencies and talents. Training provided by the enterprise is extensive and involves significant time and resource commitments. By being very selective and limiting the pool to a handpicked few, organizations adopting this strategy typically nurture, support, and take great care of their new entrants. Turnover is regarded as a significant loss and to be avoided at all costs.

Whatever the staffing strategy, Entrants want to be impressed by the company and become part of the club. They need:

♦ Training,

♦ Recognition of enthusiasm,

♦ Clear goals and performance standards,

◆ Information on how performance will be evaluated,

◆ Mentors and information resources,

◆ Expectations, priorities, and boundaries, and

◆ Frequent feedback on progress against expectations and goals.

It is the quality of the opportunity that is important to the Entrant. First impressions count here more than anything else; the quality of support as well as the relevance and effectiveness of direction provided are ingredients to successful new relationships. Because pay and benefits are agreed upon at the outset of the relationship, at this point they are not an important component to sustaining commitment and loyalty. The effectiveness of the HR staff and the speed with which tools and supplies needed to perform the job are assembled are part of the new Entrant's evaluation.

Enthusiastic commitment is sustained during the learning period through effective coaching and feedback. Through these activities, employers learn whom to keep and whom to cut. By only retaining the top performers from the Entrant group, an employer becomes branded as an exacting, high-performance organization. The organization's commitment is highly valuable to the Entrants who are kept.

HR program designs that are particularly important to this group include:

◆ New employee orientation and indoctrination,

◆ Performance management, and

◆ Training and career development.

The Contributor

The inspiration of leadership becomes increasingly important at this stage of engagement. The Contributor has demonstrated that he or she is capable of learning. Additionally, he or she has displayed enthusiasm and interest in the work.

Through selection and performance management, you know this category of employee is a leverageable resource important to your organization's success. The Contributor is using this stage of his or her career to invest in his or her own development. Loyalty and commitment to the organization can be developed by providing:

◆ Perspective,

◆ Clear goals,

◆ Frequent feedback on results,

◆ Praise,

◆ Encouragement of risk taking,

◆ Opportunities to discuss concerns, and

◆ Involvement in decision making and problem solving.

In today's tight marketplace, it is important to not become a training ground for competitors. To retain developing employees, capability pay increases are typically warranted at this stage of development. How they are distributed depends on the contributor's combination of skill growth, improved productivity, and organizational knowledge. Most typically, increases are reflected in base pay increments at this career stage level. Additionally, as the employee becomes more productive and understands more about how he or she contributes to the bottom line, interest in incentive plan participation and stock accumulation grows.

The Producer

Producers make up the bulk of the company's talent pool. They are the group of employees that the organization can quickly and easily tap for skills and organizational knowledge. They offer stability, corporate memory that sustains the culture, and an ever-important assurance of competency. They do not require intensive direction and management and are, for the most part, self-actualized. These Producers are a source of knowledge and wisdom for the Entrants and Contributors. Their sustained success requires:

◆ An approachable mentor,

◆ Clear targets and objectives,

◆ Opportunities to express concerns and participate in decision making,

◆ Support and encouragement,

◆ Praise and recognition for high levels of competence and performance,

◆ Obstacles to goal accomplishment removed, and

◆ Confidence in organizational leadership.

It is important for HR to recognize that pay, equity, and participation in organizational incentives are very important at this stage in the employment relationship. Parity with the competitive marketplace (in terms of pay, benefits, perquisites, and status) as well as opportunities for personal wealth accumulation are the symbols of commitment that employees at this career stage measure and expect. Additionally, employees at this career stage have a growing need to see alignment between their own career objectives and the corporate objectives. For this reason, selection for training and development programs related to dual career tracks, developmental assignments, executive development, and succession planning are especially valuable symbols of commitment.

The Expert

Experts possess the competencies and skills that create the brainpower and thrust to move the organization forward. Not surprisingly, they command compensation to match their skills. Experts can include those in the mid-career stage, as well as those at a later stage of their career. The key is that they have attained knowledge that makes them visionaries, innovators, role models, and centers of influence. Thus, companies are most flexible and accommodating for this group because they cannot afford to lose them.

These core individuals command the most money in the organization. They:

◆ Are sought as mentors and revered as role models,

◆ Participate in creating and implementing strategic objectives,

◆ Work cross-functional issues to solve problems,

◆ Demonstrate innovation and seek to improve technical and business competence, and

◆ Need autonomy and independence.

This elite group creates HR challenges because of their unique needs. They are motivated by:

◆ Confidence in business strategy and leadership,

◆ Desire to maintain reputation,

◆ Importance of the work, and

◆ Appreciation of others.

Research study after research study indicates that opportunities for advancement, job redesign, and learning new skills are the three non-compensation reward programs most valued by top-performing Expert employees.

Figure 4.5
HR Strategy

HR Design / Career Stage	Training, Development	Base Pay Target	Incentives and Stock	Performance Management	Benefits	Workplace
Entrant	Company orientation Assignments that provide opportunities for skill building	25th percentile of market	Hiring bonus Hiring options Incentives tied to organizational results	Clear expectations, frequent coaching and feedback Weed poor performers	Standard package with vesting period for 401(k) matches, tuition, paid time off, etc.	Work space, tools, "buddy" or mentor in place on start date
Contributor	Assignments that provide skill building and expanding opportunities	Market average Identify and reward the best with base pay increases and spot awards	Incentives tied to organizational and work unit results Performance-based distribution of options	Clear expectations, coaching, and feedback Productivity milestones Discussions about work process improvement opportunities	Standard package with full vesting in matches and valued perquisites	Opportunities to meet others Information about career programs for high performers
Producer	Developmental assignments	Between market average and 75th percentile Begin to implement designs that match individual needs	Incentives tied to individual, organizational, and work unit results Performance-based distribution of options	Participation in performance management of work group Frequent recognition Reward results	Standard package with full vesting in matches and valued perquisites	Mentors Entrants and Contributors Participation in organization-wide task forces
Expert	Leadership opportunities and projects requiring innovation and creativity	75th percentile and above Recognition and rewards that are meaningful to the individual and that create "handcuffs" to the organization	Incentives tied to individual, organizational, and work unit results Performance-based distribution of options	Participation in strategic planning of the organization Clear accountability for results	Standard package with full vesting in matches and valued perquisites	Leads projects, quality initiatives, and projects involving innovation and creativity

Creating the Winning HR Strategy

For the past few years it has been popular to start conversations on HR-related topics with the phrase: "people are our most important asset." As it turns out, research has shown that companies that have a differentiated people strategy, one that focuses on the distinct requirements of different types of employees, do perform better than companies that do not focus on people or do so in an undisciplined way. These companies back up their people strategy with human resource programs that actually reward behavior that makes the company more competitive. These companies wield a combination of policies, practices, and culture that improves the quality of their human capital and engenders true commitment from employees.

Using the career stage continuum described on the previous pages, an illustrative human resources strategy that differentiates between those gaining in skills and competencies and those who are experts can be crafted. (See Figure 4.5.)

Rewards

Determining what to pay an employee is based on the level of contribution he or she can make to the organization. Obviously, the contributions of someone whose capabilities are at the Entrant level are less than those of an Expert. Their pay position, as described in Figure 4.6, will reflect the difference between the two levels of expertise.

Figure 4.6
The Career Stage Continuum

Organizations sometimes pay Entrants a premium based on a belief that they will move more quickly through the career continuum. For example, MBAs from top schools or people with marketable technology skills command a market premium based on the potential that they will move more quickly along the career continuum. The problem with paying that market premium is that it frequently results in raising the pay level of all existing and prospective Entrants. One solution to this dilemma is to consider offering staggered bonuses to such individuals, which they earn based on meeting short-term organizational expectations.

A design for base pay and incentive plan distribution can be crafted that aligns career stage with individual contribution and performance. As illustrated in Figure 4.7, the goal is to reward those expert, top performers more than anyone else in the organization. This design delivers the correct message regarding organizational values and also helps illuminate the key drivers of competitive advantage: sustained expertise and top performance.

Instead of treating all employees to the same reward without regard to their level of contribution and expertise, the matrix considers both career stage and performance against objectives.

Figure 4.7
Aligning Career Stage with
Individual Contribution and Performance

	Entrant	Contributor	Producer	Expert
Career Stage →				
Performance Against Objectives ↓				
Top Performance	$$	$$$$	$$$$$$$	$$$$$$$$$$$
B	$	$$	$$$	$$$$$
C	0	$ (?)	$ (?)	0
Worst Performance	0	0	0	0

How Generational Differences Play a Role in Employee Motivation

Do not confuse career stage with age. The Expert can be 30 years old and the Entrant 50. Adding complexity to the notion of career stages is the fact that each generation sees life through a different filter. Generational differences color expectations, attitudes about authority, opinions about the importance of work in one's life, and general outlook on life. Four generations co-exist in today's work world. Contrast the perspective of a mature adult who grew up during the Korean War, marveling at black-and-white television and prop jets, with the viewpoint of someone immersed in cyber culture, who believes that if you can conceive it, you can create it in the digital age.

No matter what their age, in today's market, high performers and lifestylers see themselves as free agents. What is impressing many companies today is that this requires as many different deals as there are types of employees. Savvy HR professionals know that attracting and retaining the best requires targeting designs to individual interests, career stage, and needs.

Recognizing the Needs of the New Knowledge Worker

In the digital age, intellectual and human capital has taken on new meaning. Today, in the corporate value chain, data becomes information, which eventually becomes knowledge—but only if the right people are there to make it all happen. Spreadsheets and ledger sheets have no value on their own; it is how people interpret and use data and information that transforms an organization from ordinary to stellar.

Knowledge workers are central to the success of organizations. They are able to access, process, and manipulate information. Their abilities and instincts help define the culture and realize the mission. Yet, it is a mistake to dismiss knowledge workers as the domain of high-tech industry. Name an industry—construction, pe-

Figure 4.8
Changing Demographics: Generations at a Glance[4]

	Boom Echo	Generation Xers	Baby Boomers	Matures
Defining idea:	Connectivity	Diversity	Individuality	Duty
Success because:	Follow your dreams	Have two jobs	Were born, therefore a winner	Fought hard and won
Style:	Email shorthand	Entrepreneur	Self-absorbed	Team player
Rewards because:	You tried your best and succeeded	You need it	You deserve it	You've earned it
Work is:	Not amusing but it's a necessity	A difficult challenge	An exciting adventure	An inevitable obligation
Leisure is:	If I have time	Relief	The point of life	Reward for hard work
Future:	I know where I'm going; I'm just not sure how to get there	Uncertain but manageable	Now is more important	Rainy day to work for
Managing money:	Important	Hedge	Spend	Save
Education is:	A must if you want to succeed	A way to get ahead	A birthright	A dream

troleum, automotive, telecommunications, financial services, or forest products—and knowledge workers are helping to define the way work gets done and innovation takes place. Using e-mail, voicemail, mobile phones, a Web browser, and other tools, they trade information and leverage data.

These individuals are also known as *gold collar workers.* As the nature of work evolves from creating tangible/industrial goods to information-based products and services, the role of the knowledge worker becomes increasingly important. Regardless of their age or career level, knowledge workers contribute on an individual level, but their talents also combine synergistically with others on work teams to create enormous opportunities for the enterprise. Simply put, knowledge workers are the raw material that fuels the Information Age economy.

What does this mean for organizations dependent upon these workers? For one, they must understand the characteristics and needs of knowledge workers; they must fulfill their drive for accomplishment and success. For another, an organization must reward their efforts appropriately. After all, knowledge workers can take their considerable talents elsewhere, and are often inclined to do so in the pursuit of new challenges and opportunities.

Some of the needs of today's knowledge workers are:

◆ An environment that presents a high level of stimulation and challenge,

◆ Individual and organizational success, since most knowledge workers are high achievers,

◆ Technology tools, such as e-mail, workflow, Intranets, and collaboration software that facilitate group interaction,

◆ Ongoing training and education,

◆ A performance management system that measures contribution and provides mentoring and coaching,

◆ A reward and recognition system tied to performance,

◆ Influence over how and when work gets done, and

◆ Ability to balance work and family life.

In order to meet these needs, an organization must embark on a focused plan. A 1998 *Workforce* magazine survey found that 100 percent of respondents said that workers will need more problem-solving skills in the future; 95 percent said they expect the HR department to help employees develop these skills, in addition to employees developing them on their own. A whopping 98 percent believe that employees will need more interpersonal communication skills than they currently have. Add to these figures the fact that huge numbers of entry-level workers are entering the workplace ill-equipped to handle basic jobs, and it becomes glaringly apparent that learning and continuing education must rank as a top priority if organizations are to remain competitive.[5]

Knowledge sharing is also about tools—and putting them into the right hands. Today's enterprise resource planning (ERP) and human resources management systems (HRMS), as well as an array of other enterprise and personal computing technologies, allow the spread of knowledge. Corporate portals running over an Intranet allow workers to view data and information that's specifically tailored to their function or unique needs. Collaborative calendaring, project scheduling, e-mail, and documents—including word processing and spreadsheets that allow workers to track versions and threads—enable a collaborative environment that can span an office building or the globe.

But technology alone does not create a knowledge-based workplace. An organization must use the right incentives—monetary, non-monetary, and symbolic—to create a culture where people share expertise and experience. When both of these components converge, it creates an unbroken chain of knowledge transfer between individual contributors and enhances everyone's contribution, much like a relay race. Jackie Fenn, vice president and Research Director of Advanced Technologies at GartnerGroup, a Stamford, Connecticut market research and consulting firm, explains:

> If you want to develop a culture that supports learning, you first start by rewarding and promoting people who are learning continually and who are good team players who share it with each other. It's important to show that continuous learning and sharing learned experiences between contributors is observed and rewarded by management.

Finally, an organization must respect the needs of knowledge workers. Like any other group, they require targeted incentives and recognition. Unlike other groups, they also need greater autonomy and independence. Without influence over how work gets done and what work gets done, they are unable to flourish. And it's important to note that these needs extend beyond the traditional four walls of the office. Knowledge workers now demand some semblance of balance in their life. Although they might put in 60 hours a week, they want to be able to work at home, choose their hours, and turn to other innovative programs that make their lives more manageable.

Conclusion

The workplace is far different than in decades past. The dynamics of today's business environment—the various stakeholders, constituencies, attitudes, and needs—can help define an appropriate and compelling human resources strategy. Ultimately, it's about creating a great place to work, attracting the best and the brightest people, and putting all the pieces in place to create total engagement and a clear line of sight. It's about using human capital to throttle the corporate engine to full force. When all this happens, success isn't just a possibility, it's a probability.

Notes

[1] Helen Axel, "HR Executive Review—Implementing the New Employment Compact," *The Conference Board*, Vol. 4, No. 4, 1997.

[2] "WorkUSA 2000: Employee Commitment and the Bottom Line," a Watson Wyatt Worldwide Study of Employee Attitudes and Opinions, 2000.

[3] "The 100 Best Companies to Work for in America," *Fortune* magazine, January 11, 1999, Vol. 139, pp. 1-118.

[4] J. Walker Smith & Ann Clurman, *Rocking The Ages: The Yankelovich Report on Generational Marketing* (New York: HarperBusiness, 1997).

[5] "HR Predicts Future Workers Will Be Seriously Underskilled," *Workforce*, May 1998, p. 23.

The New Manager

After completing this chapter, you should be able to:

- ◆ Recognize how the role of managers has changed.
- ◆ Learn the leadership skills required to engage employees.
- ◆ Understand the role of management in building commitment.
- ◆ Create accountability.
- ◆ Communicate the "deal" to employee constituencies.

Who Is the New Manager?

In decades past, climbing the corporate ranks and becoming a manager was an accomplishment that likely brought money, respect, and power. It meant that a person had the knowledge, experience, and expertise to make important decisions that greatly affected the outcome of the business. This management model had existed for decades, largely unchanged. Its natural outcome was hierarchy—usually in the form of a command and control structure—which put a premium on directing work and controlling people and information.

Over the last decade, that model has steadily disintegrated, largely due to computers and a new generation of workers who possess more technical knowledge than their managers. Today, a Chief Executive Officer of a major company is likely to send e-mail directly to employees, meet with workers far down the corporate ladder and ask them for input, and rely on work teams to fuel new ideas and develop new products and services.

Since managers no longer control information, their role has changed. That is partly reflected in new nomenclature, in which they are sometimes referred to as "consultants" or "coaches"— terms that connote wisdom but less authority. In reality, managers must provide both the leadership and coaching needed to attract, develop, and retain talent. They must also provide the organizational memory to connect the organization of the past to the new enterprise—through the workforce. After all, in an information- and knowledge-based economy, it is *people* who distinguish a company and make it successful.

These managers are a different breed from their counterparts of the past. Today, they must act as conductors of sorts, ensuring that the various factions work together to produce a symphony rather than a cacophony. They must be short on ego, since they are almost certainly not going to receive glory and accolades, and long on patience. They also must accept the fact that they are likely to be paid less than top technical talent. Success, for these managers, is defined by a team or entire organization reaching stated goals rather than their own individual accomplishments.

What Does It Take to Manage Effectively?

One of the toughest obstacles to achieving alignment and success is molding and melding managers to fit the shape of today's horizontal structure. Without the right attitudes and the understanding of what is required in today's highly competitive, global environment, it is impossible to nurture the traits needed to realize success.

Today's manager must:

◆ **Produce in addition to manage.** Managers are respected because of the contribution, knowledge, and wisdom that are brought to the process. Today, many managers not only have the responsibility of overseeing others, they also have their own work to do. That is a sobering reality, and one that some newcomers to the ranks of management don't fully understand. Without a commitment to both "manage" and "do," personal and organizational success is threatened.

◆ **Understand the new worker's need for flexibility.** Knowledge workers won't abide by the same rules of the past, if they are to excel. A good manager understands that greater flexibility is essential, whether it relates to the hours or place one works, or the way work is performed.

◆ **Reinforce corporate strategies.** Today's manager must understand how to communicate ideas, thoughts, and goals and transform them into tangible action. He or she must also comprehend in an intuitive way how to use rewards and recognition to maximum advantage. And, perhaps most importantly, the manager must be able to articulate the vision and understand how to align work with it. Issuing orders and making threats does not succeed; motivating, while holding everyone accountable, does.

◆ **Elicit trust.** A sense of fairness and trust is an essential element in motivating workers. Even the most well-intentioned manager cannot succeed without the right set of skills. Trust is a natural outcome when a manager has the business knowledge, analytical skills, and people skills to understand the big picture and make the "right" decisions rather than play politics or feed his or her own ego.

It is no irony that today's human resources icon is Dilbert™, a cartoon character who represents nothing less than "rage against the machine" mentality. Dilbert constantly finds himself butting up against incompetent managers, in much the same way that many workers do. These problems, whether in Dilbert or in the real world, often arise from managers who confuse the concepts of control and leadership. Instead of issuing orders and commanding behavior, successful managers almost always motivate by leading workers and contribute to the creation of cohesion and pride.

◆ **Create a culture of risk takers.** Ideally a manager must balance responsibility and authority. Organizations that do not create a balance between the two risk failure. In today's workplace, managers must let decision making occur closest to the point of action. When managers do not have the authority to do so, they wind up taking on too much responsibility, and making decisions for situations they are really not prepared to handle. Even worse, they bottleneck the process. People stop making decisions and rely on them to provide a guiding light.

When managers push decision making out to others in the organization, it not only creates a sense of responsibility, it forges a new sense of empowerment. Employees begin to feel that they can affect change and implement effective solutions. They do not worry about making mistakes; they are not concerned with constantly being overruled. They're able to develop the skills required to solve problems. An effective manager never fires a person for making a bad decision; he or she fires a person for being a bad decision maker or for failing to meet expected results. Mistakes, missteps, and miscalculations are an unavoidable part of doing business.

Unfortunately, an organization that plays "not to lose" will usually fail, just as a basketball or football team that sits on the lead and plays conservatively often squanders its window of opportunity. On the other hand, if it plays to win—and takes the necessary risks—success can quickly follow. In the end, translating this philosophy into results requires that the organization holds workers, and managers, accountable for overall decision making and results rather than focusing on individual performance objectives.

Making Management More Attractive

One of the enormous challenges associated with attracting managers to this new paradigm is that it brings with it tremendous responsibility. It is easy to understand why potential managers, as well as existing ones, would shy away from a job that requires extra hours, almost no opportunity to bask in the limelight, little premium in pay, and specialized problem-solving and coaching skills.

Although it might seem tempting to toss extra money at managers, it is an issue that transcends pay. It is about respect. When a manager has the authority and responsibility to act and make decisions, respect for the individual builds. When others look up to him or her, the psychic benefits associated with leadership likewise increase.

That might sound corny, but professional fulfillment is important—especially for established professionals who are already earning a comfortable income, have achieved a measure of success, and are now looking for greater meaning in their work. In fact, as the ranks of middle management have been decimated by layoffs and downsizing, a dearth of managers qualified to coach and mentor has developed. At many companies, a vacuum in leadership exists, crippling productivity and profits.

Still, success is not guaranteed. In order for a manager to succeed, an organization must provide:

◆ **Information.** A manager who lacks solid data and information cannot make the right decisions. Today, essential data does not come only in the form of spreadsheets and business intelligence reports extracted from a database, or even an Intranet. It is information about competencies, performance measures, and more. Providing a manager with the information he or she needs to act (but not overloading the person with information that cannot be acted on) can empower the manager and lead to better decisions. That, in turn, boosts trust among employees.

◆ **A way for managers to be heard.** Nothing is more frustrating for a manager, or any employee, than feeling as though thoughts, ideas, and opinions do not count. Simply put, a disenfranchised manager is likely to spread the sense of frustration to employees like a cancer. Equally important, however, is the fact that good managers understand the situations at hand—both good and bad—before senior management ever gets a whiff.

◆ **A system of accountability.** As previously mentioned, an organization must understand who to hire, wire, and retire. Turnover that is too low wreaks havoc because it does not allow new blood to enter the organization. That can cripple vitality and the emergence of fresh ideas. On the other hand, high turnover or poorly designed HR policies can cause a brain drain that leaves the organization without adequate experience and the capability to compete. The reward system must ultimately mesh with the organization's goals. And a level of accountability must exist to flush out those who cannot contribute and reward those who add value. That in a word is "alignment," and alignment is usually a prerequisite for success.

◆ **A way to balance employee interests with management interests.** As employees put in more time, they expect greater flexibility. In Chapter **four**, we discussed the attributes of today's workplace, one of them being a more virtual work environment. Telecommuting, job-sharing, paid time off, unpaid leaves and sabbaticals, and flexible hours are all trade-offs for accepting greater responsibility and working within a performance based system. However, many successful companies are now finding even more creative ways to balance the interests of employees and management. They are initiating specialized mentoring, job rotations, and more. These firms have realized that success is a two-way street. In the end, the bottom line is ultimately tied to the front lines of the business.

When all the elements come together effectively, you can finally build a solid management structure, and develop top-notch management talent to lead the way. Those who take on the role of leaders, mentors, and coaches earn respect, help employees grow, and help rebuild a sense of clarity about career paths, rewards, and recognition—all in the context of today's business environment. Moreover, the most successful are able to advance into policy leadership roles—often joining the ranks of senior management. Within such an environment, creativity and success become reality rather than an elusive goal. People find themselves fully engaged in work and truly concerned about outcomes.

Putting an HR Strategy to Work

Effective managers find ways to make an organization's HR strategy succeed. They fundamentally understand the organization's identity, the human capital implications, what specific people capabilities bring competitive advantage, and what the "deal" is for everyone involved. They are able to sort through crucial management questions, including:

◆ How do we organize work?

◆ What capabilities does the organization need at what levels of proficiency to achieve outstanding results?

◆ Will we grow or acquire capability through strategic partnership, acquisition, or merger? When should such an event take place?

◆ What value do these capabilities add? Is it a short-term initiative or long-term? Does it boost the entire enterprise or a specific department or division?

◆ How do we organize cross-organizational resources? Who should serve on teams?

An effective performance management system can identify many of these needs. By constantly comparing an inventory of existing skills and competencies with those an organization requires, HR can create a road map of who to recruit, promote, retain, and let go. It's possible to begin molding a workforce that's aligned with the mission statement and goals. The company also can begin defining behaviors that lead to success, and using them as a guide for structuring questions during the interviewing and hiring process, as well as for coaching existing employees.

How Successful Companies Empower Managers

An organization can take many routes to arrive at the same destination. Not all of them are direct. It is important to adopt a strategy that fits the organization's philosophy, culture, and goals. At one e-commerce distribution company, management recognized that it did not have the internal expertise necessary to navigate an initial public offering and deal with the growing complexities of its industry. So, after thoroughly analyzing its situation, the firm opted to hire a second Chief Financial Officer and a second Chief Operation Officer, both with far more experience than the existing executives, to guide the company through the initial public offering (IPO) process.

Within some organizations, that might have created a huge headache. Existing executives and managers might have felt threatened, both professionally and personally. Suffering from bruised egos, they could have looked for ways to undermine the new executives. However, at this firm they understood that—with the new people at the helm—the company would win and they would win. A successful IPO would put highly valued stock in their pockets, while the executives (with previous experience at *Fortune* 100 companies) could provide valuable insights and knowledge that would benefit their careers. In fact, everyone was comfortable with the situation because the culture had been instilled with a strong desire to achieve success and to grow.

In this case, the challenge for human resources was to create a structure that would enable a successful IPO. That is only one of myriad possibilities.

At another company—a leading manufacturer of personal computers—managers are handed a "checkbook" with X number of dollars available each month. There is no need for managers to receive approval for expenditures; there is no need for a manager to justify why he or she is spending money on one item rather than another. All that counts is performance. The goal is to spend money freely but wisely, to wind up with a near zero balance at the end of the month.

Too often, organizations make multimillion-dollar commitments to clients, but require that a manager receive approval from a regional manager for a $1,000 expense. That is not consistent with empowerment, and it certainly does not give managers the flexibility to act and react in a fast-changing environment. The key, of course, is finding the right approach for a particular organization. There is no cookie-cutter method that works for all. The one constant is that all the various components required to manage—recruiting, rewards, information sharing, and accountability—must be tightly aligned. Managers must also be held accountable for the results they produce.

How Successful Organizations Develop Management Talent

According to the Institute for Employment Studies, a British-based research consultancy,[1] managerial skills typically fall into four broad domains:

♦ Organizational development and technical know-how,

♦ Conceptual and cognitive skills,

♦ Personal effectiveness, and

♦ People management skills.

Managerial skill gaps often occur because:

♦ An imbalance exists between generic and technical or functionally specific management skills,

◆ Individuals lack a high level of interpersonal effectiveness and an empowering management style, or

◆ Managers lack the ability to recognize interdependencies when managing change.

Successful organizations address the problem by focusing on:

◆ Prioritizing goals,

◆ Building relationships to maximize stakeholder value, and

◆ Motivating for performance improvements.

Communicating the Deal

Developing a compelling human resources strategy, and empowering managers, can go a long way toward achieving success. However, there is still another part of the equation: communication. Unless managers understand how to interact with various factions in the workplace, unless they recognize the needs of different constituents, an organization is likely to hit roadblocks on the path to alignment. In an era when workers are bombarded with a steady stream of messages and information, someone must translate all the noise into a cogent message.

One of the most important things managers must communicate is the concept of balanced reciprocity—that employer and employee will exchange something of value. Ultimately, that leads to the question, "What's in it for the organization and what's in it for employees?" In most cases, managers must address this issue in the context of needs, motivations, and performance expectations, for three groups:

◆ **Core Workers:** The permanent workforce is the undeniable backbone of any organization. These employees, regardless of the constituency or demographics, must be fully engaged in work at all times. In the past, when individuals signed on for a job for years, if not life, that meant providing benefits such as a generous pension to encourage and reward longevity. Today, with a growing turnover rate (the average voluntary turnover rose from 12.6% in 1997 to 13.9% in1998[2]) and with no guarantee that a specific position or job will exist in the future (let alone the company), the focus has changed. Organizations must create an environment that fosters:

1. A culture in which employees are committed to the success of the enterprise,

2. "Attachments" with employees that make them want to build a career and contribute meaningfully, and

3. A high-performance work environment where self-management and an entrepreneurial spirit are reinforced and organizational results are rewarded.

The new contract, fully supporting the notion of balanced reciprocity, says that workers will develop skills the organization needs, apply them in ways that help the organization succeed, and act in line with the new set of values. In return, the organization promises to offer engaging and stimulating work, support development of skills and competencies among employees—even if it means that they might take their talents elsewhere—and treat workers like adults. That means putting them in control of training and education through competency and performance management measures, and allowing them to handle their own retirement, stock options, and more. In the end, managers must communicate this profound change in mindset. It's far different from the models of the past.

◆ **Independent Contractors:** Companies are increasingly turning to independent contractors to fill talent needs within the organization. It is estimated that over five million independent contractors exist in the United States, and approximately 60 percent of all businesses use them at one time or another. Independent contractors run their own business, have a specialized skill, and are not directly supervised or managed while doing the work. Today, independent contractors handle computer programming, consulting, writing, photography, public relations, graphic design, Website design, law, and tax accounting and consulting.

The benefits of using independent contractors can be enormous. Contractors often offer knowledge and skills that an organization lacks. They provide greater flexibility since they can be hired for projects as needed. They can often reduce costs by cutting the need for office space, eliminating benefits, and reducing tax and legal liability. Nevertheless, if used improperly they can end up being more expensive than regular employees. For managers, the key is using these people in the right spots. If an organization becomes overly reliant on independent contractors, it can hinder engagement and alignment, since these individuals have no stake in the company. If contractors are used too sparingly, an organization might not be able to keep up with key needs.

◆ **Temporary and Part-Time Workers:** In some fields, such as health care, temporary workers have become an integral part of the labor picture. Because of short-term or ongoing staffing shortages, these individuals fill key roles. Since they are not paid directly by the company (they are usually contracted from a third-party provider), it can be difficult for managers to keep these individuals engaged and aligned. What is more, core workers sometimes resent interacting with this group because the temps have far more power in determining the hours they work and what assignments they accept.

Outsourcing and part-time work have certainly become prevalent in today's workplace. As companies begin to value knowledge over bricks and mortar, intellectual capital is the fuel that drives performance and profits. That makes it essential to develop an overall *sourcing* strategy.

Caught in the middle, however, is the manager, who must connect temporary and part-time workers to the corporate culture, and motivate them to provide the required level of service and support.

A well-defined communications strategy can engage the workforce and help the organization align itself with stated goals and objectives. When business and communications strategies are linked, employees begin to fully understand the message and can support management's objectives. Watson Wyatt has found compelling evidence that high-performance organizations rely on strong communication practices to establish guidelines, relate expectations, and explain where the organization is headed.[3]

Measuring Manager Performance

Managers, like everyone else, must be held accountable. Accountability can be determined by evaluating team results, but that alone is an insufficient measure of managerial success. Managers who achieve production results (e.g., widgets produced, projects completed, etc.) but fail to build their teams into productive units have only done part of their job. Some managers go even farther and advertently or inadvertently encourage dysfunctional team behavior.

There is an old adage, "Whipping a horse will make it go faster until it eventually dies. Nurturing it will ensure it will be around for the next race." Teams are like the proverbial horse, and managers should be judged by how they use the carrot and the stick to effectively motivate employees. Some of the relevant questions to be asked in evaluating effective management are:

◆ Does the manager's behavior foster teamwork?

◆ Is the manager respected by the team?

◆ Does the manager effectively manage performance?

◆ Are individuals given the opportunity for professional growth?

Measuring the people management side is never an easy proposition. In some instances, overt measures such as unwanted turnover may give a clue that something is wrong. Sometimes directly observable behaviors suggest either positive or negative management.

Gathering feedback from team members about a manager's performance can also shed light on managerial performance. Many companies use 360-degree performance reviews as an integral part of the managerial evaluation process. In most cases, these evaluations are conducted in the form of a survey or rating and the results are reported to the manager and to the manager's supervisor. When done appropriately, companies use the information to identify deficiencies in managerial behavior, such as the need to improve communication or coaching, and to craft specific solutions to address the issues raised.

However, the 360-degree feedback tool is one that must be used carefully. *Having subordinates evaluate their superiors can have unintended consequences. Having employees evaluate their peers and managers could have unintended consequences.* It presumes that both parties are objective and that there are no ulterior motives behind the evaluation. It also presumes that managers have broad shoulders and can willingly accept criticism. Interestingly, research suggests that companies that use 360-degree feedback do less well financially than others. *Companies must make sure that they are implementing the appropriate HR tools that are suited to their organizational goals, and will yield the desired results.*[1]

To counter these problems, some companies separate the performance review from salary decisions. This may help in specific cases, but separating the two is more easily said than done (see discussion in Chapter **eight**). In other situations, 360-degree feedback is seen as a cure for the problem of communication, rather than an information process that highlights potential issues that need to be addressed in other ways. In any event, care needs to be taken to ensure that the process is constructively administered.

Regardless of the specific system or how it is designed, the rules of the game must be perfectly clear to all players. Management must understand what is expected and how it can affect desired change. Managers' actions must revolve around articulated goals. At one major offshore bank, that translated into the statement, "Regardless of where we're based, our strategy is a global one." To support the initiative, the bank developed a recruiting system that finds individuals who are multilingual and conversant in other cultures. It also has established a performance management system that nurtures desired qualities and behaviors, and rewards those who achieve results. With the right systems in place, as well as managers who can use them effectively, the bank has grown into a global heavyweight that's respected around the world.

Conclusion

Today's managers must deal with different—some might say tougher—business conditions than their counterparts from the past. Information technology has created a highly competitive, global environment: a world where organizations must operate with the highest level of efficiency, and employees must be fully engaged in their work. Managers are a key part of the process. Ultimately, they must balance the requirements of the organization and the needs of workers. After all, managers are the ones who determine whether balanced reciprocity serves as a mere buzzword or an agent for change and, in the end, outstanding performance.

However, becoming an effective manager is no easy task. Increasingly, managers are asked to do their own work and maintain a high level of technical skill and knowledge, while overseeing others. Without the right information, rewards, and management philosophy, managers cannot motivate workers and forge a seamless link to organizational objectives and goals. Successful companies ensure that managers are empowered to make appropriate decisions, and that they possess the knowledge, skills, and tools to develop talent and create alignment.

Notes

[1] "The Human Capital Index: Linking Human Capital and Shareholder Value," Watson Wyatt Worldwide survey, 2000.

[2] P. Kettley and M. Strebler, "Changing Roles for Senior Managers," IES Report 327, 1997.

[3] "Compensation Planning for 1999," Compensation Resources Survey Information Services, 1999.

[4] "1999 Communications Study: Linking Communication with Strategy to Achieve Business Goals," Watson Wyatt and the International Association of Business Communicators (IABC).

chapter

The Role of Pay and Rewards in Boosting Company Performance

After completing this chapter, you should be able to:

- ◆ Understand how rewards contribute to organizational success.
- ◆ Describe the basic components of pay.
- ◆ Explain the different attributes of each type of pay.
- ◆ Understand how compensation affects behavior.
- ◆ Recognize what pay can and cannot do.

The Building Blocks of Success

Pay. No word evokes as much passion and consternation in the workplace. Employees sweat over wages, managers worry about granting salary increases, and executives pore over reports and spreadsheets in the quest to build streamlined and profitable pay structures. The ultimate irony—and the fact that's almost entirely overlooked—is that people don't stay with an employer or continue in a job for pay. It's all about love. When organizations get beyond providing reasonably competitive wages, pay increases communicate someone's judgment about an employee's performance, or in other words, how much they "love" the employee. Too often, managers rationalize pay distinctions made between employees by saying, "I gave the person a great pay raise, and he is still dissatisfied." A friend of ours, a lawyer, once complained that his job of managing three lawyers was the worst he ever had. He said, "when I give one a pay raise, I get three unhappy people, two whose pay didn't go up as much as the third, and one who thinks he is underpaid!" The trick is in understanding that pay is an important element in making employees feel appreciated. Employees who feel their contribution is being recognized are likely to come back day after day, even if they could be paid more elsewhere.

Companies like Oracle, Cisco Systems, and Microsoft prove that people don't work for money alone. They work for satisfaction and fulfillment. For example, Oracle has hundreds of millionaires among its 38,000 employees. Thanks to stock options, these individuals, who range from secretaries to senior managers, have been able to parlay what would have been routine pay in decades past into a highly lucrative windfall. Yet, because they remain engaged in their work and feel part of a larger and more significant process, they keep coming back for more . . . and more.

What, then, is the secret to success? Why do some companies pay less than premium wages and enjoy enormous success while others pay top scale and struggle? The answer cannot be summed up in a single word or a simple slogan. The answer lies in the complex interplay between employees and the rewards a company bestows. To be effective, those rewards must align a workforce with the corporate mission, goals, and objectives.

Make no mistake: each organization's unique mix of strategic rewards leaves an indelible mark on its workforce. Once a company has identified how to harness the required motivation, recognition, incentives, and rewards, it can design a compensation and benefits portfolio that focuses on the strategic vision. Then, and only then, is it finally possible to embrace a performance management scheme that measures and rewards desired behaviors. Only then can an organization achieve total alignment.

Beyond Money

Successful organizations understand that strategic rewards constitute more than mere pay. Strategic rewards encompass the entire work experience—from the atmosphere of the office to the size of the profit-sharing check at the end of the year. Some of these factors are recognizable and easily measured, while others operate like an ocean current. Although invisible, they can push a ship far off course. Indeed, each piece of the overall reward system plays a different role in eliciting the desired behavior, and without the right measurement tools—a corporate compass, if you will—it's questionable whether an organization can ever reach the desired destination.

A melange of compensation choices exist, and each combination is likely to lead to a different outcome. When devising a retirement plan, should an employer place a premium on years of service or an employee's direct contribution while at the company? Should it establish commissions or put a profit-sharing plan in place? Should it put a large chunk of pay at-risk or ensure that employees receive generous base pay? What about lifestyle, training, and recognition? Each of these factors, and more, has both short-term and long-term implications. Each helps mold a different culture. Ultimately, HR must take a step back and ask, "What is it we need and what role does each of our rewards and benefits play in meeting our needs?" Only then can an organization begin to align its workforce with its mission. As Edward E. Lawler III, professor of management and organization at the University of Southern California, explains:

> For a corporation to be effective, it must achieve congruency among all its operating systems. Particular practices are neither good nor bad in the abstract. Instead, they must make sense within the context of the business strategy and other systems, such as those designed to manage information, human resources, production, finance and, of course, compensation.[1]

It comes as no surprise that companies with highly effective reward systems—those closely aligned with business objectives—

invariably report superior financial results. In a 1998-1999 survey by Watson Wyatt, 36 percent of companies that align compensation plans and corporate goals do better financially. That compares to only 19 percent whose plans are "not effective"[2] and whose financial performance is less than stellar.

It's impossible to take action without understanding the types of rewards that exist. Figure 6.1 provides an overview of the types of rewards and their specific components.

Figure 6.1
Types of Rewards

Type of Reward	Components
Base Pay	Salary and basic wages
Individual and Group Incentive Pay (short-term and long-term)	Bonus; stock options; variable pay; profit sharing; signing bonus; referral bonus; etc.
Benefits	Medical, dental, and life insurance; vacation and sick days; paid time off; continuing education; dependent care; etc.
Retirement Benefits	401(k); defined contribution; defined benefit (pension)
Recognition Programs	Preferred parking; article in company newsletter; dinners; health club membership; awards; etc.
Non-Cash	Job design; training; flex-time; job sharing; compressed work week; telecommuting; etc.

What Pay Can and Cannot Do

Managers who expect remuneration to take the place of astute strategy, solid leadership, and good working conditions are not only mistaken, they're also setting themselves up for failure. In fact, an organization should alter its compensation structure only after it has designed and refined its business strategy, evaluated management, and thoroughly examined the nature of work as well as the environment in which it is conducted.

Within some organizations, a total disconnect exists among pay, performance, and expectations. Sometimes this lack of understanding can have less than obvious causes, but enormous implications. Consider the following scenario, based on a true example.

A hospital highly regarded for its level of patient care was financially solvent, despite tough regulations and a highly competitive marketplace. Nevertheless, employees had become increasingly disgruntled. In recent months, many nurses, technicians, and operations personnel had begun to voice strong support for joining a union.

Initially, senior managers were convinced that employees simply wanted more money because no one had received a pay increase for four years. The hospital administration benchmarked the hospital against industry standards and decided that the facility had to be among the highest paying employers in the region. That, management reasoned, would satisfy workers and eliminate any threat of the union.

The organization instituted an across-the-board raise of 10 percent. Workers were delighted about the pay increase, but, to the amazement and chagrin of management, the groundswell of union interest continued to grow.

Thoroughly confused, management hired consultants to sift through the situation and find a way to stave off unionization. Focus groups, interviews, and employee surveys revealed that employees had no real complaint about pay, before or after the wage increase. In fact, workers stated that because the hospital had been consistent in the application of its pay policies, it had met their expectations.

Why the growing antagonism, then? The anger centered on the workers feeling unappreciated. Employees who had three years of experience had never received a single performance evaluation. They felt as if they knocked themselves out providing quality health care but never received any feedback, good or bad. They interpreted this as lack of appreciation, and, consequently, felt a lack of connection to management. They believed the organization didn't have the same level of commitment to them as they had to the hospital.

Labor problems such as those are not uncommon. Too often, management does not have a clear idea of what pay can and cannot do. Therefore, it winds up with unrealistic expectations.

What Pay Can Do:

◆ Motivate behaviors and results.
◆ Engage employees in business success.
◆ Recognize valued skills and behaviors.
◆ Communicate commitment.
◆ Contribute to creating a compelling place to work.

Motivate Behaviors and Results

Compensation represents many things besides money. It symbolizes the employer's love and respect. It is evidence of score-keeping, and how an employee and his team stack up against the others. When it is used to stimulate activity and results, the employee's desire to accumulate that love is put to use for the organization's benefit.

A company that clearly states its objectives, establishes a well-conceived performance development program, and pays for desired behavior will motivate workers. Almost overnight, employees realize that the company places a high premium on certain actions. They begin to act in lockstep with the organization's goals. This synergy can create a powerful and formidable force that gives a company competitive advantage in the marketplace.

Engage Employees in Business Success

When pay centers on a well-conceived strategy, it's possible to achieve breakthrough results. The alignment of objectives, goals, and practices can lead to increased productivity, lower turnover, and notable gains on the bottom line. An effective performance management system linked to the overall strategic framework allows employees to feel valued.

In Watson Wyatt's 1998-1999 Survey Report, Strategic Rewards: Creating Financial Capital Through Human Capital,[4] of companies reporting excellent financial performance, 50 percent said that their reward plans were "very effective" in encouraging creating/innovation, 44 percent improved profitability, and 42 percent engaged employees in performance improvement. Organizations that base rewards on these factors are far more likely to succeed.

Recognize Valued Skills and Behaviors

The reward program is one of the most powerful ways to recognize important skills, proficiency, and demonstration of valued behaviors. Commitment and job satisfaction are in large part determined by how the reward received compares to what an employee believes he or she should receive. As such, fit is critical here. Considering the dual objectives of development and retention, the method of distribution and timing are acutely important. Too many organizations fail to recognize that employee growth and heroic performance don't occur naturally at review time or on one's employment anniversary date. The missed opportunity is always clearer with hindsight, especially when the organization is negotiating with employees' counteroffers and future promises.

Chapter **four** identifies the important levers of motivation by career stages. The following chart illustrates the most significant reward delivery medium by career stage, while considering the dual objectives of development and retention. Of course, all are appropriate rewards—the key point is to identify opportunities and create reward systems that recognize the value of human capital, reward performance excellence, and "lock up" the best of the best.

Figure 6.2
Reward Delivery Medium by Career Stage

Career Stage	Entrant	Contributor	Producer	Expert
Long-Term Incentive Designs				▓▓▓▓▓
Base Pay			▓▓▓▓▓▓▓▓▓	
Spot Bonus		▓▓▓▓▓▓▓▓▓▓▓		
Gift of Value		▓▓▓▓▓▓		
Recognition	▓▓▓▓▓▓▓▓▓▓▓▓▓			

Communicate Commitment

Pay communicates the organization's commitment to the individual. This is achieved through individual and group rewards, including spot rewards, team incentives, stock options, profit sharing, and matching 401(k) funds. It is a clear message that the organization takes its employees seriously and acknowledges their role in achieving business results.

Contribute to a Compelling Place to Work

Competitive rewards are the foundation for creating an attractive work environment. When a company links rewards to results, it aligns the culture and the business goals. Therefore, employees who contribute in a positive way and are rewarded appropriately feel valued. They reaffirm their commitment. This "halo effect" suddenly becomes a pervasive and powerful force, spurring employees to work harder and contribute more.

In order to create a compelling place to work, a company must have an overarching strategy focused on making work interesting, challenging, and enjoyable, while compensating employees in a manner that demonstrates the firm values their contributions, knowledge, and commitment.

What Pay Cannot Do:

- ◆ Create a business strategy.
- ◆ Build a corporate culture.
- ◆ Make up for poor leadership.
- ◆ Retain top performers by itself.
- ◆ Improve morale and commitment.

Cannot Create a Business Strategy

It's not unusual for a company to spend months studying, refining, and polishing its mission statement. It is not difficult to understand why. No other document defines the corporation as effectively; no other tool can focus attention and energy on the organization's goals and objectives. However, a mission statement alone cannot achieve desired results. If workers aren't given incentives and rewarded for the desired behavior, then the effort is an exercise in futility. The required behaviors simply won't emerge.

Getting to success is a major challenge. Many organizations make the mistake of relying too heavily on industry "best practices" to dictate their reward and incentive structure. Instead of assessing why a particular approach worked at a specific company, they adopt the practice without changes. Unfortunately, a best practice is a unique function of a company's management style, culture, and systems. What works for one organization won't necessarily work for another, even with the same compensation structure and management tools in place.

Cannot Build a Corporate Culture

The changing employer-employee relationship is sending shock waves through industry. As the dynamics of the marketplace and workplace change, organizations are discovering that they must also change their culture. Those that succeed understand that it is essential to use compensation to reinforce the desired cultural changes. However, pay alone cannot solve an organization's problems.

For years, companies have paid straight commissions to salespeople thinking that it would ratchet up sales by creating a monetary incentive to boost performance. But such a pay structure doesn't take into account potential problems: pushy sales associates who offend customers, and a general mistrust of coworkers who might steal leads or "close" a sale that took another associate hours to set up the day before. In some cases, the pay policy and corporate objectives conflict. Instead of sales associates working together to nurture leads and provide excellent customer care, the work environment becomes secretive, competitive, and destructive—exactly the opposite of what the company is trying to achieve.

Cannot Make up for Poor Leadership

Paying top dollar for labor sounds like a way to attract the best and the brightest. There is plenty of evidence suggesting that higher pay attracts and retains higher caliber workers, if the underlying work environment is a good one. At a company where employees are overworked, or where a dysfunctional culture exists, the fallout can be enormous. Stress-related complaints, absenteeism, and a lack of pride can ransack productivity and take a huge bite out of profits.

Cannot Retain Top Performers by Itself

Premium wages alone will not retain top performers. That depends to a great deal on the overall work environment, the nature of the job, the work team, and the portfolio of benefits and wages. If all these factors meet an employee's expectations, he or she is likely to feel satisfied and engaged.

While empirical research indicates that high pay, and particularly merit-based pay, has a positive effect on performance, unhappy and dissatisfied workers aren't likely to hang around, particularly in today's tight labor market. According to Christopher M. Lowery and M.M. Petty:

> The objective of an organization's reward system should be to retain the most valuable employees, and in order to do this, rewards must be distributed in such a way that the most valuable employees will be left with a feeling of satisfaction.[5]

Cannot Improve Morale and Commitment

Research shows that high compensation has an almost negligible effect on employee morale and commitment. According to USC's Edward Lawler:

> There is some research to suggest that high pay rates can lead to high motivation. However, motivation from this

source seems to be very short-lived. Most individuals quickly decide that they deserve whatever pay rate they receive and do not try to perform better in order to deserve it.[6]

Understanding the Compensation Continuum

Today, we constantly hear the mantra that people *are* the organization—providing the intellectual capital and brawn to fuel success. But this ongoing discussion about the "human asset" is obscured by the way many organizations behave. Too often, companies view HR as an expense—a cost of doing business—rather than an investment that can generate real gains for the enterprise.

Organizations that consider employees as investments and link rewards to outcomes often boost financial performance in ways that never seemed possible. They're able to gain tremendous competitive advantage because everyone is synchronized, similar to the way a crew rows a winning boat in competition. As a company progresses from a base pay model to more sophisticated incentives and rewards (as illustrated in Figure 6.2), it is able to drive greater results because it is also fundamentally changing the nature of work. Instead of embracing an individual and administrative mindset, it moves toward a group-focused workplace. And, in today's emerging knowledge-based economy, work teams and group problem solving are increasingly important.

Overlay work deployment and delivery with today's workforce goal for career security, and the design of effective performance management and related reward programs becomes highly complex. From the business point of view—achieving return on investment—providing career development opportunity is as much a cost of doing business as are pay and benefits, as Figure 6.3 illustrates. The good news is the construct also matches the personal goals of today's employees.

Figure 6.3

The linkage of strategic business needs—achieving results and building capacity—with the reward continuum provides the foundation for the effective design of a strategic rewards program. Base pay can help an organization acquire capability, leading to increased skill development and ultimately to increased organizational capacity to produce goods and services. Using a combination of base pay and a mix of strategic rewards such as spot awards, bonuses, and short- and long-term incentives, leads to increased organizational performance and better results, as illustrated in Figure 6.4.

Figure 6.4

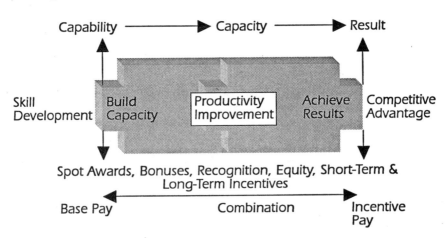

Base Pay

Base pay serves as the economic foundation for work. It is rooted in market dynamics and reflects the basic value for a person's skills. In other words, there's usually little flexibility in determining basic compensation because employers are bound by what other organizations pay for similar talent. Companies, of course, do have the choice of paying below, at, or above the prevailing market wage.

Base pay plays an important role in building a compensation system. Ted Turnasella, compensation manager for *Newsday*, put it this way:

> Base pay motivates in two ways—one positive, the other negative. When employees know that another job carries another base pay, they are motivated to work toward a promotion. At the same time, because base pay compensates for being competent, workers will maintain competence or risk losing their jobs.[7]

Base pay isn't a static tool, however. Companies use a variety of means to ensure that they remain competitive. The most interesting shift in today's delivery of base pay is the toggle between job-based and person-based pay.

♦ Job-based pay: Reward level set based on the job as determined by the competitive market—not the person.

♦ Person-based pay: Reward levels are based on the competitive market, the incumbent's unique combination of skills and competencies, and the criticality of the person to the work environment.

This change is reflective of the flattening of organizations; instead of increasing pay through hierarchical promotions, people are rewarded for their expanding skills and proficiencies with the "market" as a reference. On the reverse side, instead of paying "market rates" for persons who lack full skills and proficiencies, the organization provides "opportunity" for development. Think roles—not jobs.

Competency and Skill-Based Rewards

Competency and skill-based rewards are for the most part person-based rewards. For example, a young lawyer who passes the bar exam possesses value, despite the fact that he or she has never actually practiced law. At this point in the young attorney's career, he or she is worth X dollars in the marketplace. The figure might vary slightly, but it will certainly fall into a given range, based on what all employers are willing to pay. Yet, after this fledgling attorney executes one or two wills, and then handles probate for an entire will, he or she creates greater value for the employer. The individual's contribution changes because of the breadth and depth of experience.

In today's business environment, you can use tools that can actually measure the skills and capabilities of employees. Competency-based management systems are a common method for coaching and tracking results. In some cases, the system might exist as a paper-based evaluation or rating system. In other instances, an organization might use a software solution that ties into succession planning, training, and compensation data. The key is to put some type of measurement in place.

For a reward structure to work, an organization must focus on the capabilities it needs; inventory existing capabilities; identify the gap between what it has and what it requires; build systems to educate or train workers; and determine which employees have expanded their capabilities and reward them appropriately.

Recognition

Recognition reinforces desired behaviors. It follows performance and acknowledges outstanding results. Some types of recognition are formal, such as an award for an outstanding employee; other types are informal, including verbal recognition, or cash or cash-substitute awards handed out close to the time of performance. The power of recognition can't be overstated. People always perform better when given positive reinforcement.

Recognition plans underwrite the performance management process. They are a profound way of saying "thank you" and showing workers that the organization values their efforts and contributions. And when spirits rise, productivity usually follows.

Successful employee recognition plans:

♦ Recognize employees for behaviors that contribute to outcomes.

♦ Link to business needs and to incentive plans for internal consistency.

♦ May have monetary or symbolic rewards.

♦ Should allow for multiple types of recognition.

Realize, however, that different types of recognition produce far different results. For instance, formal, visible awards establish role models throughout the enterprise. Informal rewards create a sense of accomplishment for individuals. Equally important—and often overlooked—is the day-to-day, verbal recognition that creates and reinforces culture. Because many employees have limited upward potential within an organization, the positive feedback they receive can keep them on track and motivated.

Some examples of effective recognition programs include:

♦ Outstanding employee award,

♦ Days off,

♦ Special activities or events,

♦ Letters or phone calls from top executives,

- ◆ Parking spot,

- ◆ Magazine subscription,

- ◆ Special lunch or dinner,

- ◆ Upgraded computer equipment,

- ◆ Tickets to movies or sporting events,

- ◆ Participation on task force or special committee, and

- ◆ Contribution to a favorite charity.

Incentives

Incentives are distinctly different from recognition. Instead of "recognizing" someone for past behavior that exceeds expectations and then rewarding them, incentives motivate individuals to engage in specific behavior that coincides with the organization's goals and objectives. Simply put, recognition is a link to the past, while incentives are an attempt to influence future performance. A conceptual relationship of pay and performance is displayed below.

Incentives engage employees in business improvement. The more interdependent the work is to the accomplishment of results, the more likely it is that group incentives will smooth internal competition. Still, group incentives tend not to recognize individual contribution, whether good or bad. In contrast, individual incentives reward and promote employee contribution, and minimize group achievement. The more independent the work, the more important it is to link metrics, contribution, and reward. Figure 6.5 illustrates the incentive pay continuum, from fixed to variable pay; the performance expectations of each approach; and their pros and cons.

Figure 6.5
The Incentive Pay Design Continuum

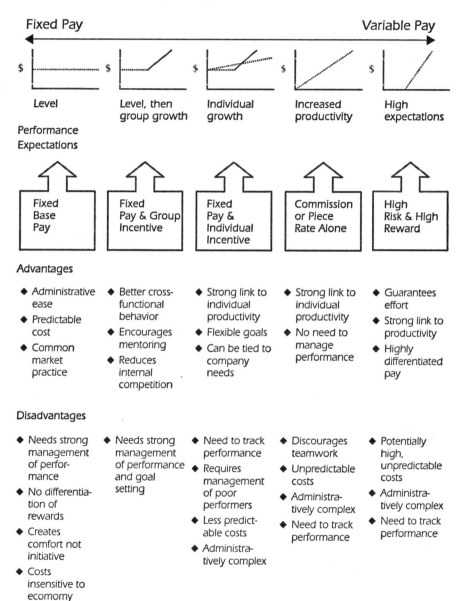

Level	Level, then group growth	Individual growth	Increased productivity	High expectations

Performance
Expectations

Fixed Base Pay	Fixed Pay & Group Incentive	Fixed Pay & Individual Incentive	Commission or Piece Rate Alone	High Risk & High Reward

Advantages

◆ Administrative ease	◆ Better cross-functional behavior	◆ Strong link to individual productivity	◆ Strong link to individual productivity	◆ Guarantees effort
◆ Predictable cost	◆ Encourages mentoring	◆ Flexible goals	◆ No need to manage performance	◆ Strong link to productivity
◆ Common market practice	◆ Reduces internal competition	◆ Can be tied to company needs		◆ Highly differentiated pay

Disadvantages

◆ Needs strong management of perfor-mance	◆ Needs strong management of performance and goal setting	◆ Need to track performance	◆ Discourages teamwork	◆ Potentially high, unpredictable costs
◆ No differentia-tion of rewards		◆ Requires management of poor performers	◆ Unpredictable costs	◆ Administra-tively complex
◆ Creates comfort not initiative		◆ Less predict-able costs	◆ Administra-tively complex	◆ Need to track performance
◆ Costs insensitive to ecomomy		◆ Administra-tively complex	◆ Need to track performance	

In an environment in which group incentives are the primary form of variable pay, it is important to recognize strong performance and to deal with non-contributors. On the other hand, where individual incentives are used, the organization needs to make a commitment to differentiating performance and rewards, but to look for opportunities to minimize competition. Many companies use a combination of group and individual incentives to moderate the negatives of both approaches. As with all compromises, this lessens the positive effect of both types of plans, while reducing the negatives associated with each. In truth, there is no hard-and-fast rule. Each organization has to structure its pay design in a way that best serves business strategy, desired behaviors, and organizational culture.

Of course, individuals, groups, and teams within organizations display all kinds of behaviors, some desirable and some not. By identifying these action points and developing the proper incentives, it's possible to influence actions and effect organization change. Whether there's a need for greater information sharing, a broader skill base, more teamwork, or a focus on total customer care, the incentives ultimately drive behavior. A basic but profound truth that bears restating is that *you cannot change organizational culture until you change behavior.*

Individual, group, and team incentives can produce significantly different outcomes, yet all are an essential part of an organization's human resources strategy. While each requires some form of measurement or metrics to identify whether a program is working effectively, a strategy can be engineered in many different ways.

In the book *1001 Ways to Reward Employees*, Bob Nelson offers the following example of an organization with a well-conceived incentive program:

> Cellular One . . . awards car phone installers $10 for every customer compliment they get (mostly on customer comment cards) and deducts $10 every time a customer complains about an installation and $20 if a vehicle is damaged during the installation. Vehicle damage has fallen by 70 percent, and customer compliments have tripled since the company began the operation.[9]

Individual Incentives

Individual employee incentive plans are characterized as follows:

- ◆ They differ from bonuses. They have rules established up front and often include a discretionary component.

- ◆ Once the domain of executives, they are now used among the entire workforce.

- ◆ They can support team efforts.

- ◆ They link pay with individual performance, whereas group incentives tie compensation to team performance.

Group and Team Incentives

Group incentives have their own characteristics:

- ◆ They can band together formerly disparate groups of employees and create a common goal.

- ◆ They can drive cultural change more rapidly.

- ◆ They reinforce the interactive and dependent nature of work.

- ◆ They can be used at all levels of the organization.

The key point is to differentiate between different performance levels by developing attainable incentives that match organization goals. Within that context, employers can use all sorts of targets when devising an incentive program. The key issue is to create valid targets. For example, sales incentives tie pay to sales volume. Gain-sharing plans tie pay to unit performance. Profit-sharing plans build a sense of ownership in the business by letting everyone share in the organization's success.

It's crucial for an organization to create realistic performance objectives and goals. If the barriers or thresholds are set so high that year after year there's no payout, the organization loses credibility. If the barriers are set too low, so that everyone achieves the threshold, they no longer serve as an incentive. Instead, they become an entitlement, and in some cases, workers begin to perceive them as part of base pay. Adjusting and tweaking team incentives to reflect the organization's requirements—and changing needs—is essential. Organizations that succeed invariably understand the dynamics of their company, industry, and marketplace.

At that point, organizations can fully engage employees in their work because the bottom line is in their line of sight. Suddenly, they can see the correlation between their actions and organizational outcomes. They can understand in a tangible way that their contribution leads to gain. Still, the task of aligning goals and outcomes doesn't get any easier. Once workers have an unobstructed line of site, organizational credibility can face a huge test. Employees suddenly become critical business partners who make it a point to understand their work. And they feel empowered to make decisions that affect the business outcome.

Does all this mean that the right rewards and incentives can produce any result we want? Absolutely not. Pay is only one part of the rewards universe. The highest salary and most progressive incentives alone cannot keep a person engaged, employed over an extended period, and in sync with the organization's goals, vision, and business mission. That requires understanding the power of pay and what it can and cannot do.

Conclusion

Strategic rewards help shape an organization. It's essential to understand the types of rewards, how and where they can be used, and how they affect the mindset of individuals, teams, and groups. Yet, while compensation is the centerpiece of a successful corporate business strategy, it alone cannot guide a company to outstanding performance and profits. Nothing can replace a highly focused business strategy and a commitment to making a workplace challenging and rewarding. However, when pay supposts business goals resultling in total alignment, world-class results are within reach.

Notes

1 Edward E. Lawler III, "The New Pay: A Strategic Approach," *Compensation and Benefits Review*, Vol. 27, July 17, 1995, p. 14(9).

2 Strategic Rewards®: Creating Financial Capital Through Human Capital, Watson Wyatt Survey Report, p. 2, 1998/99.

3 Jerry L. McAdams, *The Reward Plan Advantage: A Manager's Guide to Improving Business Performance Through People* (San Francisco: Jossey-Bass, 1996).

4 Strategic Rewards®: Creating Financial Capital Through Human Capital, Watson Wyatt Survey Report, p. 2, 1998/99.

5 Christopher M. Lowery, M.M. Petty and James W. Thompson, "Employee Perceptions of the Effectiveness of a Performance-Based Pay Program in a Large Public Utility," *Public Personnel Management,* Vol. 24, No. 4, Winter 1995, p. 476.

6 Edward E. Lawler III, *Strategic Pay: Aligning Organizational Strategies and Pay Systems* (San Francisco: Jossey-Bass, 1990).

7 Ted Turnasella, "Aligning Pay with Business Strategies and Cultural Values," *Compensation and Benefits Review*, Vol. 26, 1994, pp. 65-68.

8 McAdams, p. 119.

9 Bob Nelson, *1001 Ways to Reward Employees* (New York: Workman Publishing Co., 1994).

chapter seven

Performance Management and the Strategy of Rewarding People

After completing this chapter, you should be able to:

- ◆ Understand the link between an effective performance management system and competitive advantage.
- ◆ Construct an effective performance management system.
- ◆ Align designs with business goals and strategy.

Performance Management Defined

Performance management establishes the overall direction for a company, from the top to the bottom, and defines how it will get there. In the macro sense, it is the business strategy translated into operating plans; in the micro sense, it is the setting of group, team, and individual goals. Winning companies incorporate the performance management process into day-to-day operations.

As organizations have moved from command and control structures to nimble, market-driven constructs, competitive advantage has been won through technical excellence, innovation, speed, quality, and customer service. In order to raise the bar of employee performance, organizations have built tools to improve productivity and personal ownership of development and growth. As we've discussed, high-performance organizations have recognized that performance can best be achieved through alignment.

The Many Faces of Alignment

There is an old saying, "If you don't know where you're going, any path will take you there." Organizations that closely monitor productivity are far more likely to wind up with employees who pay attention to output. Those that emphasize and measure customer service are likely to produce workers who think about how they can satisfy customers or clients. And those that promote and measure creativity and innovation tend to achieve superior results that derive from innovation. As we noted in Chapter **three**, if something is important, measure it; if it is very important, reward those individuals who measure up.

Alignment is more than just monitoring, measuring, and remunerating. It's the sum total of corporate culture, goals, vision, and business practices—and how an organization communicates and translates all of these to its workers. It's the company's commitment to providing a high quality of work life, flexibility, a stimulating environment, opportunities for career development, and the "right" portfolio of benefits that creates true alignment. Again, when the entire "crew" rows as one unit rather than as disparate individuals, the group moves in the right direction with tremendous velocity. Other organizations might be paddling faster and harder, but if their workers are not rowing together, they are not getting to the finish line as quickly.

Understanding how different elements of strategy interact to produce alignment is critical. Figure 7.1 breaks down these elements into four functional categories.

The *navigation*[1] *system* helps employees understand the business goals and what they as individuals, teams, or departments need to do to reach those goals. It includes formal communications about

Figure 7.1

How Human Resource Programs Link to Company Strategy

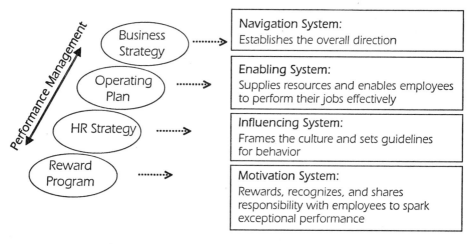

goals and objectives, such as the chairman's or president's message to employees, company newsletters, and other forms of updates on progress toward goals. It also includes informal communications, such as sharing information between departments and open employee meetings. Performance management programs, reviews, and other interactions involving day-to-day performance planning, problem solving, and coaching are all part of the navigation system.

Organizations enable the workforce by providing tools, equipment, information, and resources to do their jobs. Tangible elements of the *enabling system* include access to technology as well as education and development opportunities. Organizations also enable their employees by empowering them to make decisions about their work, to solve problems, and to collaborate with coworkers.

The *influencing system* that helps create a corporate culture is probably the most difficult of the systems to identify and measure. Elements include norms and valued behaviors, rules of conduct, and cues that employees use to shape the way they treat customers and each other. It is the "how" part of the job. While company goals play a part in the influencing system, the real drivers are the deeds—how senior management and middle management support company goals by what they say and how they do it. High performance organizations have used competency management and re-lated tools to identify organizational needs and gaps, and to coach, build, and reinforce desired behaviors and actions.

Rewards and recognition are the cornerstones of *motivation systems*. Motivation systems also relate to employee job satisfaction. Programs and policies related to job satisfaction include the level of autonomy and responsibility employees have to do their jobs, involvement of employees in the policies that affect them, and the opportunities to enhance job satisfaction by learning new skills and opportunities.

Performance management is critical to running a business and is a core process. It has the following characteristics:

◆ Performance is optimized when all systems—navigation through motivation—are aligned with corporate goals.

◆ Performance management is not about controlling employ-ees; it is about creating partnerships based upon mutual re-spect and trust.

◆ Accountability and personal self-management are embed-ded into processes and designs.

Traditional performance management programs have placed most of their emphasis on planning and assessment, and little, if any, emphasis on execution. Moreover, traditional programs have been "owned" by the HR department. In high-performance organiza-tions, performance management is owned by management; em-ployee objectives are set in context with larger organizational strat-egies; and the process is facilitated by simple, understandable, easy-to-use tools that can help managers improve performance and en-able individual employees to become self-managing. Because per-formance management is embedded in the important day-to-day actions of the organization, interdependent, cross-organizational goals and accomplishments as well as functional goals are shared.

Building an Effective Performance Management System

Effective performance management programs are built to serve the organization. As such, there is no pattern or formula to copy. Figure 7.2 maps the important architectural components of a performance management process.

Figure 7.2
The Performance Management Process

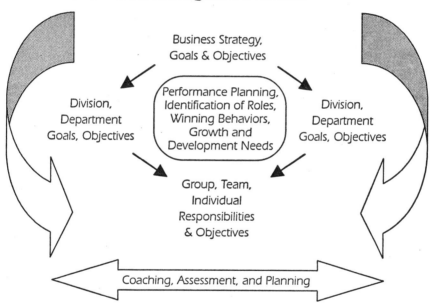

Performance management is the process for focusing individuals and groups on the larger organizational goals. In every instance, it involves:

◆ Planning,

◆ Setting expectations,

- ◆ Observing results,

- ◆ Measuring,

- ◆ Coaching,

- ◆ Evaluating, and

- ◆ Rewarding.

Over the last few years, leading management thinkers have developed a variety of concepts to help organizations optimize the value of their people. Two of the most compelling concepts are that human capital is a necessary and expandable resource and that competencies can be used as both a map and a measure for the growth of human capital.

The Role of Competencies in Performance Management

In Chapter **four**, we described the career stage development of individual employees. Each individual follows the path from Entrant to Contributor to Producer to Expert. Building individual competence, however, contrasts with building organizational competency. The former describes the range of skill acquisition as an individual grows into a job or job class. The latter describes what the organization needs to build the capability and capacity to support corporate strategy. From the organization's view, defining specific competencies necessary for its growth and organizing them in a way that identifies individual career milestones allows it to build its organizational competency, while providing employees with a clear career path. Competencies reinforce the specific behaviors necessary for business success.

As organizations have become streamlined and flatter, measures of success and growth have changed. For many companies, the development of competencies and professional growth within a job have replaced "climbing the corporate ladder." It is not surprising that competency-based performance management designs have been adopted by high-performing organizations. Often referred to as role profiles or career bands, organizational competencies provide a framework for grouping jobs into meaningful levels based on role and competency expectations. They provide flexibility in managing employee development, performance, and pay. The advantages are numerous, since they:

♦ Articulate what the organization values,

♦ Provide a common language for employees and managers to describe value creation,

♦ Establish organizational roles to support cross-organizational functionality, collaboration, and teamwork,

♦ Provide a tool for resource planning, training, and recruitment,

♦ Provide employees with greater role clarity and a map of career paths,

♦ Provide a tool for job leveling—as opposed to salary administration grades,

♦ Guide employees and managers as to what is expected even in times of dramatic change and restructuring,

♦ Are easy to implement and administer, and

♦ Provide an integrating platform for HR programs (see Figure 7.3).

Figure 7.3
Using Competencies
to Integrate Different HR Programs

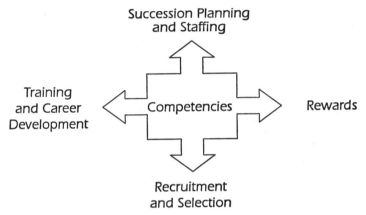

When combined with functional job descriptions, the foundation for individual performance planning, coaching, and appraising is created.

Organizational Competencies answer the questions:	Job Descriptions answer the questions:
What behaviors and applied competencies are most important to business success?	What are the primary duties and accountabilities? What are the skills and technical qualifications expected?
How should employees approach their work?	What skills must be acquired to move into another job? What are lateral opportunities and what are promotional opportunities?
What can employees expect from their peers? From their supervisors? From leaders?	
What are future needs in terms of staffing and succession planning?	
What are the competencies we should be developing?	

Developing Organizational Competencies

Developing organizational competencies begins with identifying general competency categories and valued behaviors that are a necessary prerequisite for organizational success. Watson Wyatt Worldwide research indicates that the number one competency identified by both high-performing and other companies is technical knowledge. This is followed by skills related to interpersonal relationships and leadership—communication and decision making, ability to lead and manage, and flexibility and adaptability.

Despite the overall unanimity about critical competencies, there is some variance by industry, as shown in Figure 7.4.

Figure 7.4
Variance in Critical Competencies by Industry

Manufacturing	High Tech	Health Care	Energy	Finance	Services
Organizational skills	Interpersonal skills	Analytical skills	Organizational skills	Ability to influence	Ability to influence
Creativity	Ability to influence	Knowledge of business	Technical knowledge	Ability to lead and manage	Interpersonal skills
Ability to deal with ambiguity	Technical knowledge	Willingness to learn	Flexibility	Creativity	Technical knowledge
Ability to influence and persuade	Flexibility	Ability to lead and manage	Willingness to learn	Technical knowledge	Ability to deal with ambiguity
Communication skills	Ability to lead and manage		Ability to influence		

Competencies such as these are further segmented by levels of professional achievement. Thus, an individual at first is expected to contribute his or her expertise. As he or she matures professionally, the nature of the contribution changes to guiding other less-experienced individuals in making their organizational contribution. Finally, the career continuum moves from "Guiding" as a principle, to "Leading" the organization and its people. A typical competency format is displayed in Figure 7.5.

Figure 7.5
Competency Model for Technology Firm

	Contributing		Guiding		Leading	
Performance Factors	Profile 1	Profile 2	Profile 3	Profile 4	Profile 5	Profile 6
Technical Excellence	Uses basic knowledge associated with role Provides support with supervision Gains knowledge of work area, services/ products	Uses working level skills/ knowledge within work team to resolve moderately complex issues Displays basic knowledge of services/ products outside work area Provides support with limited supervision	Able to use skills/ knowledge in cross-functional situations Independently provides comprehensive services Understands relationships of products/ services across the organization Communicates complex information to wide variety of employees	Recognized as internal expert in profession Leverages skills/ knowledge to improve current practice Communicates complex knowledge in strategic context Resolves complex issues Serves as resource to others	Achieves technical objectives representing major organizational contribution Uses advanced communication skills to facilitate negotiation of complex issues Independently originates new concepts and approaches	Demonstrates broad business knowledge/ perspective Identifies organization-wide issues and supports resolution
Customer Service	Understands importance of customer satisfaction Sensitive to customer needs Commitment to quality service but needs guidance	Ability to partner with customers and anticipates some needs Seeks customer feedback Understands how performance impacts customer satisfaction	Ability to understand and anticipate customer needs Coordinates with others to address customer issues Uses customer feedback to improve product/ service delivery Assumes responsibility as part of broader work group for meeting customer expectations	Knowledge of customer's business and strategy Suggests improvements to product/ service delivery model Identifies new opportunities to satisfy evolving customer needs	Takes lead in improving customer product/ service delivery model	Sets tone for customer service and quality

Figure 7.5 continued

| | Contributing | | Guiding | | Leading | |
Performance Factors	Profile 1	Profile 2	Profile 3	Profile 4	Profile 5	Profile 6
Interpersonal Skills & Teamwork	Shares information effectively Follows through with commitments Works effectively and consistently as part of a team Displays integrity and respect for the views of others	Contributes constructively to team solidarity Supports issue resolution within team Provides guidance/ coaching to more junior colleagues Delegates tasks	Consistently contributes to team issue resolution Uses communication skills to influence decisions Reinforces team decisions Collaborates with team members to develop new ideas Provides constructive performance feedback	Recognized as mediator Evaluates performance; identifies additional skills, training, experience in team members Ensures integration of work across departments Establishes networks which facilitate overall client delivery	Serves as advisor, providing guidance for others outside direct reporting relationship Supports collaboration across business units Models desired behaviors and serves as an enabler of corporate strategies	Establishes organizational vision/ strategies Sets tone supporting: collaboration, communication, valued behaviors, and integrity Models desired behaviors Builds relationships across organization and with customers
Decision-Making	Understands strategy and operating objectives Uses judgment as to when to seek assistance Makes decisions regarding own work Schedules own time	Understands division and corporate strategies Uses independent judgment Makes recommendations about department work	Begins to influence strategy and/ or marketing Judgment impacts own work and immediate work group	Contributes to business strategy Identifies trends Judgment to resolve complex issues Makes decisions that impact work unit	Develops strategies that respond to market Sets strategy for business unit Resolves complex issues Decisions impact business	Defines organizational performance indicators required to determine success Contributes to major corporate strategy Helps to align/ strengthen organizational capabilities Helps determine need for corporate acquisitions, mergers, initiatives, etc. Decisions impact company

Figure 7.5 continued

Performance Factors	Contributing		Guiding		Leading	
	Profile 1	Profile 2	Profile 3	Profile 4	Profile 5	Profile 6
Leadership	Accepts guidance from managers & leaders	Gives limited guidance to others Sets example for entry-level workers	Serves as a resource for others Provides constructive performance feedback Acts as a champion for products/ services Ability to lead projects	Identifies needed skills, training, etc. in others Primary resource for other unit employees Implements business strategy for unit Mentors wide range of employees Aids development/ implementa- tion of policies/ procedures	Evaluates performance of subord- inates; Advises/ provides career development Helps develop, motivate, and inspire others Models organizational vision, valued behaviors, and principles	Assesses performance of senior managers Manages largest corporate units Establishes vision, values, and principles and models behaviors Proposes/ champions successful organization- wide initiatives Establishes/ supports vision and strategies
Project Management	Prioritizes work on concurrent assignments	Defines steps/ estimates times for small projects and for parts of larger projects	Defines task, resources, and time for medium to large projects	Gains cooperation/ commitment from others on multi- discipline projects Designs/directs to completion big integrated projects	Manages major projects or internal initiatives involving multiple work areas and departments	

The Performance Management Process

The performance management process has three distinctive steps: planning, coaching, and evaluating.

Planning: Functional job descriptions and organizational competencies combine to create performance expectations. At the beginning of the performance cycle, the manager and employee agree on important results and discuss the organizational roles, competencies, and behaviors important for business success.

Coaching: Throughout the performance cycle, the employee and manager meet to discuss progress, priorities, and performance. In today's busy workplace, these meetings are often employee initiated, but are more positively received if the coach/manager calls the meeting.

Evaluating: The organizational competencies are used to discuss performance accomplishment.

Figure 7.6 is a sample form that combines all three of these elements.

Figure 7.6
ABC Medical Group Performance Development Plan

This form includes the following sections:
Section I: Performance Standards
Section II: ABC Success Qualities
Section III: Overall Evaluation Summary
Section IV: Development Plan
Section V: Coaching and Feedback Record

To be Completed by the Manager

Employee Name:

Social Security #:

Position Title:

Current Profile: ____A   ____B   ____C   ____D
(check one)

Department Name:

Manager's Name

Manager's Title:

Review Period: From   To

For any failed competencies, a plan for improvement should be created under Section IV: Development Plan.
(A second testing of the competency should be included as a part of the employee's improvement plan.)

Review of Credentials
Check one box for each query:
1. Copy of current licensure in dept file?   Yes____ NA____
2. Copy of current certification in dept file? Yes____NA____
3. Copy of current CPR card in file?   Yes____NA____

Education/Training Review
The employee has attended the following:
1. Confidentiality   Yes____No____NA____
2. Quality Improvement Yes____No____NA____
3. Position Specific Educational Activities
                            Yes____No____NA____

Figure 7.6 continued

Section I: Performance Standards
(To be discussed at the beginning of the performance cycle and assessed at the end of the performance cycle)

In this section, performance standards can be either: a) listed in the space provided below, or b) referenced from the job description. (If the job description is referenced, please attach a copy to this form.) Please check with pen/pencil the corresponding for the 3-4 priority standards which rate MOST IMPORTANT when considering all of the job's duties and responsibilities. **The standard for ABC Medical Excellence is contained in ABC Success Qualities (Section II) and does NOT need to be listed below.**

1. _____

| Unacceptable | Developing | Competent | Proficient | Outstanding |

Comments: _____

2. _____

| Unacceptable | Developing | Competent | Proficient | Outstanding |

Comments: _____

3. _____

| Unacceptable | Developing | Competent | Proficient | Outstanding |

Comments: _____

4. _____

| Unacceptable | Developing | Competent | Proficient | Outstanding |

Comments: _____

5. _____

| Unacceptable | Developing | Competent | Proficient | Outstanding |

Comments: _____

6. _____

| Unacceptable | Developing | Competent | Proficient | Outstanding |

Comments: _____

7. _____

| Unacceptable | Developing | Competent | Proficient | Outstanding |

Comments: _____

8. _____

Form Date 5/98

Figure 7.6 continued

Section I: Performance Standards
(To be discussed at the beginning of the performance cycle and assessed at the end of the performance cycle)

	Unacceptable	Developing	Competent	Proficient	Outstanding

Comments: _____

_____

Form Date 5/98

Figure 7.6 continued

Section II: ABC Success Qualities
(To be discussed at the beginning of the performance cycle and assessed at the end of the performance cycle)

Profiles describe contribution expectations within ABC. Each profile is built around a distinct set of Success Qualities that characterize positions within the same profile. ABC Success Qualities are specific skills, abilities, valued behaviors and customer service skills that determine individual as well as ABC Medical Center success. For a specific description of the ABC Success Qualities for your profile, refer to the Profile Model.

TECHNICAL EXCELLENCE: Possesses skills and technical competence to execute job duties. Operates within policies and procedures. Adheres to health/safety standards.

| Unacceptable | Developing | Competent | Proficient | Outstanding |

Comments:

_____

_____

INNOVATION, PROBLEM SOLVING & FLEXIBILITY: Identifies problems, secures relevant data to identify possible causes. Generates alternative courses of action and possible consequences, welcoming input from others. Actively seeks opportunities to improve and embraces new ways of operating.

| Unacceptable | Developing | Competent | Proficient | Outstanding |

Comments:

_____

_____

BUSINESS LITERACY: Understands customer needs. Manages own work and/or the work of others in ways that exceed customer expectations. Acts in ways that enhance organization's financial and customer service performance.

| Unacceptable | Developing | Competent | Proficient | Outstanding |

Comments:

_____

_____

PERSONAL PERFORMANCE & VALUED BEHAVIORS: Demonstrates and encourages ABC mission of courtesy, respect and compassion in all interactions. Strives to resolve interpersonal conflicts, promoting positive working relationships. Takes the initiative in situations, while displaying prudent judgment. Actively participates in individual performance improvement and evaluation.

| Unacceptable | Developing | Competent | Proficient | Outstanding |

Comments:

_____

_____

Evaluation Criteria:

Unacceptable	Developing	Competent	Proficient	Outstanding
Performance does not meet job requirements. An action plan has been created to address areas needing improvement.	Employee has demonstrated some competency; however, results do not consistently meet job requirements. An action plan has been created to address areas needing improvement.	Results are good. Performance is consistent with job requirements.	Results often exceed job requirements. Employee consistently demonstrates skill in meeting job requirements and can be used as a role model/mentor on a local (departmental) level.	Results significantly exceed job requirements. Employee consistently demonstrates that he/she is an expert in meeting job requirements and can be used as a role model/mentor on an organizational (multidepartmental) level.

4

Figure 7.6 continued

Section III: Overall Evaluation Summary
(To be completed at the end of the performance cycle)

The purpose of this section is to provide an overall assessment of performance over the previous period regarding all performance standards and ABC Success Qualities.

In selecting an Overall Evaluation, the evaluator should consider:
- The importance of the job performance standards to the job and performance results
- The ratings for the job performance standards
- The ratings for the Success Qualities

The Overall Evaluation Summary selected should best describe the level of performance exhibited by the employee on a consistent basis when considering all of the performance standards and ABC Success Qualities.

To receive one of the five Overall Evaluation Summary categories:

The **majority** of the evaluated elements in Sections I and II must fall into that particular category or higher
(Majority is defined as more than half)

If the employee is rated "unacceptable" in any category, the overall evaluation cannot exceed "competent".

Unacceptable	Developing	Competent	Proficient	Outstanding
Performance does not meet job requirements. An action plan has been created to address areas needing improvement.	Employee has demonstrated some competency; however, results do not consistently meet job requirements. An action plan has been created to address areas needing improvement.	Results are good. Performance is consistent with job requirements.	Results often exceed job requirements. Employee consistently demonstrates skill in meeting job requirements and can be used as a role model/mentor on a local (departmental) level.	Results significantly exceed job requirements. Employee consistently demonstrates that he/she is an expert in meeting job requirements and can be used as a role model/mentor on an organizational (multidepartmental) level.

Manager's Comments:

Employee's Comments:
The section is for the employee to provide written comments regarding the completed Performance Planning and Development Form. Filling out this section is optional. The comments will not change the manager's comments or ratings, however, they will become part of the employee's performance record.

Form Date 5/98

Figure 7.6 continued

Section IV: Development Plan
(To be developed at the beginning of the performance cycle, reviewed during the course of the performance cycle and updated at the end of the performance cycle)

In the left hand column, identify skills critical to meeting your job's performance standards, the ABC Success Qualities for your profile, and/or expected results for the next twelve months. In the middle column, outline an action plan to address each area to be developed. Results from the action plan should be documented in the right hand column.

Areas listed in this section may include:
- Skills needing improvement as identified in job duties (Section I: Performance Standards)
- Areas needing improvement as identified in your profile (Section II: ABC Success Qualities)
- Incomplete or new goals
- Skills or areas that will lead to growth in job responsibilities and/or profile

Areas Targeted for Development	Action Plan	Results Achieved

SIGNATURES INDICATE COMPLETION OF THE PERFORMANCE PLANNING AND DEVELOPMENT FORM

Manager's Signature_____   Date_____

Employee's Signature_____   Date_____

Form Date 5/98

Figure 7.6 continued

Section V: Coaching and Feedback Record
(To be used, as needed, over the course of the performance cycle)

This section should be used during the course of the performance cycle to record feedback regarding performance, conversations regarding the development plan and/or clarifications to job expectations. The purpose of this record is to document such discussions between the manager and the employee.

In lieu of writing in the space provided below, other forms of documentation may be attached to this tool such as e-mail messages and Performance Improvement Plans (PIPs). All written communication should identify the date and the person completing the documentation.

Feedback Highlights

Notes/Observations   **Documented by/Date**

_____   _____/_____

_____
_____
_____
_____
_____
_____
_____
_____   _____/_____
_____
_____
_____
_____
_____
_____
_____   _____/_____
_____
_____
_____
_____
_____
_____

7   **Form Date 5/98**

Figure 7.6 continued

Instructions

A. The Performance Development Cycle at a Glance

Performance Planning

The Process	*The Timing*
Identify performance standards using the job description and related documentation. The manager documents specific duties, responsibilities and expected results in Section I. (The 3-4 most important standards should be highlighted as indicated in Section I.)	For new hires, transfers or promotions: Within first month of hire
Review ABC Success Qualities for the profile associated with the job. The manager identifies the job's profile, referring to Section II of this form and the ABC Success Qualities Profile Model.	For other employees: Planning for upcoming performance cycle can occur at the time of the performance appraisal
Establish the employee's Development Plan. The manager and employee complete Section IV of this form.	

Coaching and Feedback

The Process	*The Timing*
Assess progress toward achievement of the Development Plan. The manager and employee refer to the Development Plan in Section IV, updating it as appropriate.	As appropriate during the course of the performance period
Discuss employee's performance in relation to the job's performance standards and ABC Success Qualities profile. The manager (or manager designee) completes Section V of this form as necessary. This section can be updated throughout the performance period, serving as an on-going documentation record.	

Performance Appraisal

The Process	*The Timing*
Assess results achieved. The manager evaluates the employee using Sections I and II of this form. Comments should be provided by the manager to illustrate performance evaluation ratings.	At the end of the performance period
Assign overall evaluation category. The manager completes Section III. Comments should be provided by the manager to illustrate the Overall Evaluation Summary rating.	
Discuss performance appraisal with employee. Upon completion of Sections I, II and III, the manager and the employee should discuss the evaluation ratings and comments for these sections. The employee may elect to comment in the space provided on page 4.	
Review and update Development Plan. The manager and employee discuss progress regarding the Development Plan. The manager updates Section IV of this form as appropriate.	
Sign the completed form. The manager and the employee should sign and date the completed form on page 5.	
Communicate salary adjustment as appropriate. The manager completes the Employee Change Form, indicating the performance appraisal completion date, employee rating, salary adjustment and the effective date of salary adjustment. Also, the manager indicates if the "above maximum" adjustment applies. The manager communicates all of this information to the employee. Manager e-mails the completed Employee Change Form to Human Resources.	
Plan for upcoming performance cycle. The manager updates the performance standards and Development Plan for the upcoming performance period. The manager reviews this information and the ABC Success Qualities with the employee.	

Figure 7.6 continued

Instructions

B. Purpose of the Form

The Performance Planning and Development Form is used for:
- Confirming job roles and responsibilities,
- Evaluating and documenting performance,
- Discussing career development, and
- Facilitating communication during the performance development process.

C. Responsibilities of the Manager AND the Employee in the Performance Development Process

In general:
- Be familiar with the forms and tools to be used for performance development.
- Come prepared when participating in performance discussions.
- Understand the performance standards and the ABC Success Qualities profile for the job under discussion.
- Ask questions.
- Actively participate in discussions using examples to support and illustrate your ideas.

To make the process as effective and rewarding as possible and encourage a more constructive and meaningful dialogue, the manager and the employee should:
- Each independently review the appropriate sections of the form. **Using this form, the employee should conduct a self-appraisal of their own performance.**
- Schedule opportunities to discuss performance, including planning, feedback and appraisal.

D. Evaluation Criteria

Unacceptable: Performance does not meet job requirements. An action plan has been created to address areas needing improvement.

Developing: Employee has demonstrated some competency; however, results do not consistently meet job requirements. An action plan has been created to address areas needing improvement.

Competent: Results are good. Performance is consistent with job requirements.

Proficient: Results often exceed job requirements. Employee consistently demonstrates skill in meeting job requirements and can be used as a role model/mentor on a local (departmental) level.

Outstanding: Results significantly exceed job requirements. Employee consistently demonstrates that he/she is an expert in meeting job requirements and can be used as a role model/mentor on an organizational (multidepartmental) level.

The manager should retain the originals of all completed forms and the employee should receive a copy. For questions on the performance development process, consult your manager.

9

Form Date 5/98

Linking Rewards

More than anything else, a reward strategy must reinforce the desired behaviors and actions. It must bring an organization together and create greater synergy among individuals. Working with the various rewards available—including base pay, incentives, benefits, retirement benefits, and recognition and non-cash rewards (see Chapter **six**)—employers can create a compensation strategy that fits a particular constituency and career stage.

Base pay is perhaps the easiest piece of the puzzle. After all, it is relatively simple to check wage surveys and make a pay decision based on "market conditions" and "competitive requirements." Base pay, as previously indicated, is really nothing more than what a company must pay to play. Merit increases, step-rate increases, and general wage adjustments do little or nothing to motivate workers to share in team and enterprise goals.

The bigger issue is how the compensation framework fits with the performance management system.

In competency-based organizations, mangers are responsible for making pay decisions that support business needs as guided by consideration of:

◆ Performance against established objectives,

◆ Development,

◆ Current pay in relation to market, and

◆ Budget.

Competitive positioning of rewards is often population specific, and ranges are designed around the market average and 75th quartile of comparator organizations. As described in Chapter **four**, career stage and level of contribution then are used to position total rewards appropriately. Figure 7.7 illustrates compensation positioning by career stage.

Figure 7.7
Market Positioning by Career Stage

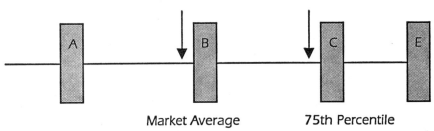

Market Average   75th Percentile

Total Compensation Positioning
A: Entrant
B: Contributor
C: Producer
E: Expert

As the individual's value to the organization grows over time, so does his or her positioning within each pay level. The matrix in Figure 7.8 provides a conceptual framework for pay increase decisions that integrates both career stage and competency development.

Figure 7.8
Performance Matrix

| | | Competency Development | | | |
	Performance	Entrant	Contributor	Producer	Expert
Performance	Top	$$	$$$	$$$$	$$$$$$
Against	Middle	$	$$	$$$	$$$
Objectives	Bottom	0	0	0	0

case study

Building the Performance Development Model

A leading online service provider recently adopted the performance matrix approach in managing its employees. To retain industry leadership in an intensely competitive area, characterized by hyper-growth and talent shortages, the company decided to redesign its performance development model around the competency approach described above. The goal of the new performance management program was to:

♦ Align individual and team performance around critical business issues,

♦ Reinforce the existing culture of self-management and entrepreneurship, and

♦ Manage ongoing performance using a new performance management approach.

Competencies similar to ones illustrated above were developed using company-specific Success Profiles, ranging from one to six. These reflected both the common attributes of similar organizations, such as technical excellence, teamwork, and interpersonal and business skills, as well as company-specific attributes that positively distinguished it from its competitors. Things such as customer service, initiative, and self-management were felt to be keys to the company's present and future business success. Using Success Profiles and related performance management tools, managers evaluated individual performance against established goals and professional development.

As part of the design process, the company developed a rigorous job analysis procedure to build job content descriptors that were meaningful for market pay comparison and benchmarking, recruitment, internal posting, and employee development planning. The result was a range of information that could be used to compare each job with other positions in the company and with similar positions in the marketplace. This, in turn, provided a basis for building the company's compensation model.

Linking Pay to Performance

The process produced market pay ranges, which specified the base salary opportunity for a particular job.

An individual's salary was set within a given range based on his or her performance and skill development as described in Figure 7.9.

Figure 7.9
Determining Pay

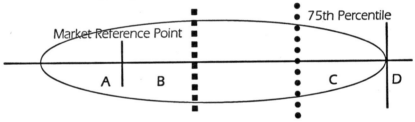

Employee Profile	Target Range Placement
A. New/Developing Employee or Employee not Achieving Expectations	Up to 90%
B. Proficient Employee Meeting Expectations	90% - 110%
C. Highly Proficient Employee Consistently Exceeding Expectations	110% - 120%
D. Recognized Expert Demonstration Sustained High Performance	120% +

The company also developed Promotion and Job Movement guidelines that aided managers in determining appropriate pay changes for movement within a success profile, movement to a higher level profile, or simply a lateral job move. While administering salaries using this approach is data intensive, modern software greatly simplified the process.

The company's compensation management framework achieved a number of desired goals:

◆ Clearly identified skills, values, and behaviors, which were important to the company's success,

◆ Competitive pay ranges, which supported company goals of attraction and retention of talent, and

◆ Flexibility, permitting an individual's pay to be differentiated based on performance and skill development, and business needs.

In the end, the company's new pay approach aligned individual contributions with organizational needs, making winners out of everyone.

Conclusion

Results are produced by the cumulative effect of all of an organization's programs. Analysis of financial data shows that companies with aligned performance management programs perform better in the marketplace. Such programs help focus the organization and all the individuals in it on what they can do to add value to the organization. All programs—business strategy, operating plans, staffing, development, and rewards—are aligned when the behaviors elicited by the performance management process support the overall mission of building the organization's competencies.

Notes

1 "Alignment; The Last Frontier for Creating Competitive Advantage," Watson Wyatt Worldwide study, 1997.
2 "The Human Capital Index: Linking Human Capital and Shareholder Value," Watson Wyatt Worldwide survey, 2000.

chapter

Building the HR Brand: The Attributes of Winning Organizations

After completing this chapter, you should be able to:

- ◆ Use the power of a human resources strategy.
- ◆ Build a competent workforce.
- ◆ Use communications to build commitment to business strategy.
- ◆ Build a human resource brand.

The Attributes of Successful Companies

Great companies do not just happen. In fact, luck does not play a sustaining role in business. It is opportunity, vision, and planning that make an organization successful. Moreover, world-class enterprises are always in a state of transformation. They are constantly striving to be the best.

Think about Cisco Systems, Dell Computer, America Online, and Merck as examples of organizations that constantly redefine success. They entered the world to seize specific market opportunities. Visionary in their leadership, they created products and business processes that could build ever-greater momentum. None of this was serendipity. It took vision, strategic planning, careful implementation, measurement, and continual retooling and recalibrating to ensure that these companies stayed on course.

Successful companies share specific attributes:

◆ A well-articulated human resource philosophy and strategy,

◆ A committed, competent workforce,

◆ Relentless communication, and

◆ An "HR brand."

Their success is not an accident, and it's not alchemy, either. The trick is to create a road map to guide employees through continual transformation.

Creating an Articulated Human Resource Strategy

It sounds obvious, maybe even simple. However, articulating a meaningful human resource strategy is one of the most critical, and challenging, first steps in creating or transforming a department or an entire organization. A clearly defined approach is more easily translated to stakeholders, converted into a workable plan, and measured accurately. That ultimately makes it more feasible to implement.

The philosophy underlying the HR strategy is rooted in the business case, though it is derived directly from the mission statement. It is important to consider these questions when articulating a human resource philosophy and strategy:

◆ What is your business plan?

◆ Who are your competitors?

◆ What are the implications of your short-term and long-term plans?

◆ What kinds of employees do you need to fulfill your business mission?

◆ What attracts these types of employees?

◆ What are the constraints or barriers you face?

◆ What are you going to do to differentiate yourself?

Figures 8.1 and 8.2 demonstrate how, in two companies, in two different industries, diverse internal and external factors ultimately translate into differing key human resource strategies.

The actual human resource strategy can be established in any number of ways. The strategy can be expressed in a single document, segregated into mission, values, and corporate goals, or it can be unveiled piecemeal and rolled out over time. In some cases, it begins as a direct communication via video or in person to employees. In any case, communicating only once is not enough.

The strategy filters extraneous activities, and prioritizes corporate activities. Establishing the company maxim is only the first, and in some respects, the easy part. The hard part is gaining consensus throughout the organization. To do this requires "selling" and not just "telling." Convincing senior management and heads of business units is often the toughest but most necessary job. These individuals provide validation about the power and accuracy of the strategy, and they need to be won over early in the process.

Change for most people is traumatic. Human inertia dictates that most people accept a routine and resist getting out of it—especially if there is no compelling reason. Samuel Johnson once observed that nothing focuses the mind more than a good hanging. Likewise, the threat of impending financial or other doom tends to focus employee attention and can be the catalyst for a change in direction. We can all name companies that found themselves in dire straits and were able to change strategic direction.

Figure 8.1
Human Resources Strategy: Technology Firm

Internal: Who Do We Want to Be?	External: Business Environment
◆ Employer of choice ◆ Center of excellence ◆ Market dominant ◆ 20% annual growth	◆ Unique core product ◆ Core business under continental siege by competitors ◆ Extreme competition for new and existing talent

Translating internal and external factors: What does this mean?

◆ Engaged, supportive work environment
◆ Personal self-management
◆ Customer-absorbed
◆ Individual responsibility for professional development
◆ Continuous improvement protocols
◆ Team-based activities

Key Elements of Human Resource Strategy

◆ Motivate cross-organizational collaboration and teamwork
◆ Facilitate skill, knowledge, and capability growth through career pathing, training, and development opportunities
◆ Market-based competitive reward and benefits
◆ Emphasis on results and value creation by linking group and individual performance goals with business strategies
◆ Reward experience and know-how
◆ Reward efforts that significantly exceed expectations

Figure 8.2
Human Resources Strategy: Institutional Bank

Internal: Who Do We Want to Be?	External: Business Environment
◆ Growing financially ◆ An innovator of new products, services, and markets ◆ Strong customer relationships ◆ Skilled workforce	◆ Competition squeezing margins ◆ Competition for talented employees

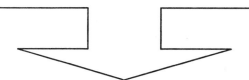

Translating internal and external factors: What does this mean?

◆ Optimize small, capable workforce
◆ Emphasis on versatility and cross-organizational integration and learning
◆ Customer focus depends on employee stability
◆ Need to communicate roles and expectations

Key Elements of Human Resource Strategy

◆ Establish programs that focus on improving customer relationships
◆ Move away from the notion of "jobs" to "roles"
◆ Identify/create valued behaviors that emphasize leadership, teamwork, and cross-organizational cooperation
◆ Ensure competitive pay and bonuses; continually review internal pay practices to make sure they stay relevant to job markets
◆ Team rewards tied to business performance and identified improvement
◆ Individual rewards tied to competencies and contribution

Barring threatening circumstances, however, employees need to be persuaded that the new vision is worth their commitment. Gaining commitment to the new strategy is a prerequisite for its successful execution, no matter what the job market looks like. Simply being honest and open about why a new direction is necessary is generally the best place to start winning over employees. Corporate communications must give employees a sense of what will be demanded of them by the new strategy and why. In instances where downsizing will be necessary, assuring employees that they will be fairly treated is critical.

As noted in earlier chapters, human resource professionals have a key role to play both in establishing the new vision and in developing plans, programs, and policies that support and reinforce consistent behavior. Using a variety of tools, such as focus groups, networking, surveys, and meetings, HR professionals can help communicate the new direction and to process employee feedback. Once people within the organization can support the new direction, HR design must reinforce the message through training and development, communication strategies, and reward policies.

The following two examples illustrate the power of an articulated strategy in the overall HR design.

case study

Human Resource Strategy at Global Oil[1]

Global Oil is a 100-year-old company that had a long tradition of providing career employment. During the 1980s, the company's economic fortunes turned downward, requiring the company to reduce its employee population for the first time. After repeated downsizing resulting in great internal trauma and huge severance costs, company management decided that it needed to change its human resource approach. As a first step, they looked at their employment needs going forward and divided the employee population into two types. The first was the core of employees essential to keep the company going through all economic environments. These individuals could range from senior management to critical refinery personnel. A second group included workers to whom Global could not commit to career employment. Some of these individuals were professionals who met a specific need for the company, but because they were professionals, their skills could be used by any industry competitor. Engineers, geologists, and other "petro-techs" fit into this category. Many of these workers work for relatively short periods of time for one company and, when demand for their services slackens, they move on to other companies. Even so, the ability to attract and retain these individuals at the right time is critical. Similarly, the unpredictability of the refining business made refinery worker jobs less secure than in the past.

The company announced that career employment could no longer be guaranteed, but that employees who left or were terminated would be treated fairly. The company also redesigned its HR program from one that penalized shorter service employees to one that balanced the needs of both shorter and longer service personnel.

In this case, the articulated strategy required:

- ◆ A solid core of career employees supplemented by a flexible ring of specialized professionals and non-skilled workers, who would come and go at the company's or their own choice,

- ◆ Fair pay for an individual's contribution, but no promise of career employment,

- ◆ Pay for performance,

- ◆ No company-imposed retention barriers, such as long vesting schedules or retirement or health benefits that were earned only after long service,

- ◆ Ratably accrued benefits, such as a plan in which one unit of work equals one unit of retirement or an equal portion of the company retiree health care subsidy,

- ◆ Enhanced portability of benefits, and

♦ Special incentive plans to retain a limited number of select employees.

Designing the HR program meant putting in place:

♦ A cash balance plan, which provided equal benefit accruals and lump-sum benefits,

♦ A redesigned company 401(k) plan with expanded eligibility, shortened vesting, and an increased employer's matching contribution,

♦ A retiree medical plan that vested individuals in the company portion of its contribution based on his/her number of years of service,

♦ A severance package that recognized the company contribution to portable retirement benefits, and

♦ A long-term incentive plan that rewarded selected managers for improvement in shareholder value and a targeted bonus program to retain critical talent.

The defining ideas were fairness and portability. The cost of increasing the company benefits was offset, in part, by reducing the "lost-benefit" make-up allowances, previously included as part of the severance package. The company proceeded to shorten eligibility periods for joining various benefit programs, including health insurance and paid time off, to help attract new employees. The company also amended its plans to permit lump-sum payouts of benefits and rollover of accumulated savings from and to other companies' plans. Underlying the strategy was the belief that if you treated employees fairly they would want to stay, but that there would be few impediments to leaving. While such a human resource strategy seems almost quaint in today's competitive labor market, at the time it made sense to a company facing repeated downsizing and an uncertain future.

case study

Human Resource Strategy at Bank of the World[2]

Picture the senior management team of a small offshore bank, sitting around the boardroom table discussing their unique business case. They sift through the business issues and the people issues, considering all issues from a variety of angles.

The business problem is twofold: first, to identify the rights and privileges of being an executive at the bank; and second, to entice executives to move around the world as needed. Clearly, human resources strategy is key to the bank's long-term prosperity. Equally important is the ability to explain the bank's vision in a way that all stakeholders will understand and embrace.

The bank leadership is global—based in different countries around the world—thus making it essential to develop an equitable reward and salary structure. For example, the organization must pay executives living in Mexico City and Luxembourg who perform similar roles in a way that ensures equity. This concept became a core value. It ultimately helped motivate executives to become global players, and that led to greater global synergy. The bank came up with the strategy: "Regardless of where our managerial talent is located, Bank of the World's global strategy provides equal benefits." This was expressed in the bank's adopted philosophy, shown in Figure 8.3.

Figure 8.3
Bank of the World's HR Philosophy

Strategy	Design and Operating Guidelines
◆ Attract/Retain highly-skilled staff	◆ Attract/retain local staff complement.
◆ Motivate staff to high levels of performance and productivity	◆ Value jobs considering the labor market, responsibilities, skills, and scope of assignment. Starting salaries are based on individual qualifications. Salary growth is commensurate with performance, productivity, increased experience, and responsibility.
◆ Maintain standard of excellence in conduct of business	◆ Maintain flexible administrative practices, consistent with organizational objectives of equity and fairness, which recognize the variability of human resource and compensation policies in the different international labor markets in which the bank operates.
◆ Reward individual staff members for demonstrated performance	◆ Periodically reward staff for performance, contributions, and other significant accomplishments.
◆ Be fair and equitable with staff	◆ Ensure that base compensation program remains competitive in relation to banking industry and local standards at the 75th percentile.
	◆ Provide career opportunities through training, transfer, and promotion options by:
	◆ Promoting continuing education through tuition reimbursement
	◆ Providing in-bank training programs
	◆ Encouraging lateral transfers and promotional assignments.
	◆ Encourage understanding of human resource and performance pay policies by making staff aware of human resource policies, position descriptions, performance objectives, and salary ranges through continuous and consistent communications.

Building a Committed Workforce

There are four steps to building a committed, competent workforce: recruiting selectively, building organizational competency, managing performance, and enhancing capability.

1. Recruiting Selectively

The first step in building a competent workforce is to recruit the right people. Research by Watson Wyatt Worldwide underscores the importance of recruiting excellence. In the survey of 405 companies described in Chapter **two**, paying attention to the hiring process seemed to pay real dividends. Paying attention, in this case, meant:

- ◆ Professional new hires, well-equipped to perform duties,

- ◆ Recruiting efforts specifically designed to support the business plan,

- ◆ Employee input into hiring decisions, and

- ◆ A formal recruiting strategy.

Companies that did a good job in these areas critical to the hiring process were associated with a cumulative 10-percent increase in market value!

As a first step, managers need to address the following question: "What does the firm need to gain a competitive advantage?" In order to create a useful profile, it's crucial to first define the ideal employee's characteristics. Which of the following is most important?

- Creativity,

- Leadership,

- Verbal communication skills, or

- Congenial personality?

Which characteristics will contribute the most to the success of the organization?

- Is excellence important? If so, how will you measure it during the hiring process? College GPA? Relevant experience? References? How do you build a performance management system around excellence so that you continually have the best people available for specific business needs?

- Are experience and expertise important? What sources do you use to ensure that what the individual appears to offer exists in reality? Skill tests, references, degrees, writing samples, etc., provide some guidance, but are not always an accurate predictor of how the individual will perform on the job.

- Are client commitment and customer service key attributes? If yes, how will you measure these qualities when recruiting and hiring? What specific questions should you ask during behavioral interviews in order to obtain this type of information?

- Is the ability to think analytically key? Typical interviewing might not provide any insight. You might need a writing sample to evaluate how a candidate constructs and organizes thoughts.

If an organization is to hire people who can negotiate the corporate culture, an organization must balance what it needs with what will fit. Too often, employers hire new employees based solely on predefined skill sets necessary to occupy a specific job. In the haste to fill openings, they overlook the key question: "How will the person fit into the organization?" Almost without exception, a company can teach a reasonably smart individual to master a specific skill set. Rarely, however, can it reshape an individual's personality and behavior. Unfortunately, the result is often an individual whose behaviors don't contribute to the organization's business goals. No amount of money or training will succeed in aligning that individual with company strategies or objectives.

In theory, a distinction exists between recruitment and selection. *Recruitment* is the process of attracting qualified and interested individuals to fill available job vacancies. *Selection*, in contrast, is the decision-making process aimed at identifying those persons most able and willing to meet the organizational expectations as to performance and professional growth. In practice this distinction is often blurred, but its importance lies in understanding the need to develop approaches around both activities, which will help you hire the right people in a timely manner.[3]

Some companies are biased against moving existing employees into new positions. As one manager reminded us, "You're never a prophet in your own land." Instead, internal recruitment should be a priority. Promoting from within helps to ensure positions are filled by employees who are aligned with the organization's business goals and are used to its culture. When a firm starts with a promote-from-within mindset, it lets employees know that new skills and competencies will further their careers and reinforces their importance to the organization. Employees who have climbed the corporate ladder can provide experience and expertise, while reinforcing the culture and history of the organization. They become a valuable resource to others, frequently serving as mentors or role models for younger employees. Moreover, an organization that demonstrates its willingness to promote its employees implicitly communicates that it values its internal talent. Even at a time when the "job for life" philosophy has vanished, a hire-from-within approach lends stability to an organization in the midst of change.

There are times, of course, when an organization needs to look outside its existing talent pool for new employees. These circumstances include situations where:

◆ Necessary skills or experience are not available internally,

◆ Existing or expected workloads cannot be maintained by current employees, and/or

◆ Cultural change will be aided by the addition of employees with different perspectives that are aligned with the new organization's goal.

Whether recruitment is internal or external, one of the most important lessons is to establish selection criteria and stick to the decision—even when faced with organizational pressure to fill a job quickly. Too often in the rush to fill a position, employers will bow to staffing pressures and hire someone who doesn't fit the organizational profile. Obviously, some staffing decisions need to be made quickly to ensure continuity of the organization. But as another author notes, this "get me a warm body" scenario is, unfortunately, all too typical and illustrates many of the problems and realities involved in recruiting for a position.[4]

Even when employers hire individuals who possess the necessary skills to fulfill the position, they may still not fit the organizational profile established as part of the selection process. The individual, too, finds himself or herself trapped in a position from which there is no advancement, or worse, from which he or she leaves within a relatively short period of time, forcing the hiring process to begin anew. As a result, the goal of building organizational competency goes unserved.

The better strategy is for organizations to continuously identify and hire talented entry-level employees. We at Watson Wyatt frequently deal with organizations that have demographic holes in their profile. As middle managers retire or sometimes leave, companies lose valuable experience and managerial talent that cannot easily be replaced.

To accommodate an ongoing recruitment process requires planning ahead. It also means building an effective recruitment and selection process. However, hiring talented individuals is only part of the process. An organization must also commit to developing employee careers with the idea that some will one day fill higher-level positions. To create this kind of framework requires identifying and building organizational competencies and effectively managing individual performance.

2. Building Organizational Competency

In Chapter **four**, we described the career stage development of individual employees. Each individual follows the path from Entrant to Contributor to Producer to Expert. We also noted in Chapter **seven** that building individual competence, however, contrasts with building organizational competency. The former describes the range of skill acquisition as an individual grows into a job or job class. The latter describes what the organization needs to build the capability and capacity to support corporate strategy. From the organization's view, defining specific competencies necessary for its growth and organizing them in a way that identifies individual career milestones allows it to build its organizational competency, while providing employees with a clear career path. This clarity doesn't go unappreciated. Competencies provide employees with a common language of career development and reinforce the specific behaviors necessary for business success. In the end, everyone wins.

As we have previously discussed, competitive wages, incentive pay, and targeted benefits constitute strategic rewards that can have enormous power to effect change within an organization, if they are tied to business strategy. As discussed in Chapter **seven**, building a solid competency-based platform around business needs is an essential starting point in creating the link between employee achievement and business success. By implicitly communicating desired behaviors, key employees understand their roles in the organization, are motivated to achieve greater professional success, and are aligned with the business strategy.

Research clearly supports the importance of linking rewards to performance and to business strategy. Rewarding top performers more than average performers, linking pay to a company's business strategy, and paying above market are all significantly associated with success in the marketplace. Similarly, using performance appraisals to set individual pay is also linked to bottom-line success.[5]

3. Managing Performance

In Chapter **seven**, we discussed using competencies as a basis for linking behavior to business goals. Actually, managing performance is equally critical. It includes coaching, evaluating, and rewarding individual performance to ensure employees are attaining personal and organizational targets. The goals are threefold:

◆ To ensure that functional roles and job duties are performed in a satisfactory manner,

◆ To reward performance that is aligned with desired organizational roles and valued behaviors, and

◆ To provide an annual measure of an individual's professional growth.

These goals interact to create performance objectives, as illustrated in Figure 8.4.

Figure 8.4
Setting Performance Expectations

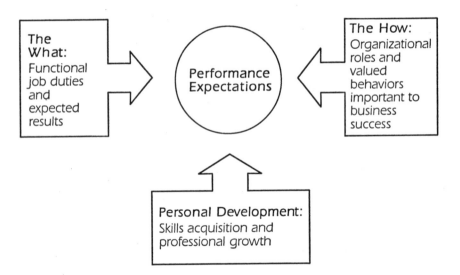

The What: Functional job duties and expected results

Performance Expectations

The How: Organizational roles and valued behaviors important to business success

Personal Development: Skills acquisition and professional growth

While many treatises have been written about the performance appraisal, it is worthwhile to summarize the process here. At the beginning of each performance cycle, managers or coaches need to set forth specific expectations regarding functional job requirements, valued behaviors, and individual growth opportunities and memorialize these in a performance management plan (see Chapter **seven**). As part of this process, the individual needs to understand the expectations surrounding his performance in his job (e.g., moving from Entrant to Contributor as discussed in Chapter **four**), the expectations associated with organizational competencies, and the weight associated with each. These performance expectations, once set, should provide the individual with a clear understanding of his or her goals and how to achieve them. During the course of the year, the individual's performance to date should be discussed—no employee should be surprised by his final evaluation. The year-end appraisal includes an evaluation against the initial performance plan. Incentive pay awards, advancement opportunities, and developmental needs are determined based on this final review.

Even though intuition and empirical information identify the importance of linking pay to performance against company goals, it is curious that some companies separate the performance review process from pay decisions. The argument is that separating the two encourages greater focus on individual growth. This approach is flawed. Pay is the most effective way of incenting desired behaviors. By removing it from the performance review process, employers undercut their own ability to encourage positive alignment with company goals and strategies. It also takes away the legitimate rationale for the pay decisions that ultimately have to be made in any regard. In reality, most employers really do use performance in making pay decisions, despite protests to the contrary. Saying the two are separate simply encourages cynicism on the employees' part, and winds up being a demotivator.

4. Enhancing Competency

Good people stay with high-performing firms if they believe in the organization, in its management, and in the opportunity to fully develop their talents. According to a 1998 employee survey, only 14 percent of employees receiving training at work indicated they would change employers in the next year. In contrast, 24 percent of those not receiving training anticipated changing jobs.[6] Other research supports that opportunities for advancement are the most effective non-pay reason cited by employees for being attracted to or staying in a job.[7]

Jeffrey Pfeffer, in his book entitled *Competitive Advantage Through People: Unleashing the Power of the Work Force*, cites two good examples of the impact training can have on an organization:

> At a Collins and Aikman carpet plant in Georgia, more than a third of the employees were high school dropouts, and some could neither read nor write. When the firm introduced computers to increase productive efficiency, however, it chose not to replace its existing work force, but to upgrade employees' skills. After spending about $1,200 per employee on training including lost job time, the company found that the amount of carpet stitched increased 10%. Moreover, quality problems declined by half. The employees, with more skills and better morale, submitted some 1,230 suggestions, and absenteeism fell almost by half. At Hampden Papers, a paper mill, the organization began spending 1.97% of the total payroll on education and training. Although productivity benefits were difficult to quantify, the president of the firm noted that "workers who take part in classes have lower rates of absenteeism and job turnover. They also tend to get higher performance ratings from their supervisors."[8]

Training and development are at the core of strategic alignment. Not only is training crucial for an organization that wishes to remain competitive, it helps satisfy the desire of today's worker to maintain a high level of employability. It offers a symbiotic benefit for the organization and the employee by creating a framework for performance management.

But training done badly can have a negative impact on the organization and, in some cases, is associated with a negative financial impact. The Watson Wyatt survey (Human Capital Index) mentioned earlier found that market values were significantly less for those companies that reported: (1) that training is provided to employees for attaining higher level positions, and (2) that training programs are maintained even in less than favorable economic circumstances. Pfeffer offers one explanation for this:

> Training will produce positive returns only if the trained workers are then permitted to employ their skills. One mistake many organizations make is to upgrade the skills of both managers and workers, but not change the structure of work in ways that permit people to do anything different. Under such circumstances, it is little wonder that training has no apparent effect.[9]

In our experience, training is often non-specific and, as Pfeffer's comments suggest, not immediately translatable into day-to-day work. Such programs seek to enhance program skills, but have ill-defined personal application. Where training is linked to either professional achievement (e.g., a degree or valuable professional certification) or to new skills that aid in increasing one's abilities to perform the job they are doing or are going to do in the near future, training can build not only employee skills, but commitment as well.

While training benefits individual employees by increasing their career stage expertise, organizations also benefit by using it to develop workforce competency. Some even use the completion of designated training programs as a milestone within the competency matrix. One firm we know suffered from poor project management skills among its employees. As a result, the firm developed its own course in project management and linked promotion to the attainment of a higher band level. The result was an improvement in managing large projects by those who had this responsibility and a greater appreciation of the need to support project management techniques by the non-project managers.

Relentless Communication

A great vision, a fine program, and an excellent HR design rely heavily on a comprehensive communications campaign if they are to succeed. It is a complex challenge to take all of the factors that make a best-of-class organization and communicate them proactively throughout the company, particularly in a way that engages the workforce. Yet, only when business and communications strategies are linked can employees begin to fully understand and act on key messages. Figure 8.5 provides some critical communication attributes.

Figure 8.5
Methods for Effective Communication[10]

Explaining New Programs in the Organization	68%
Helping Employees Understand Business Goals	67%
Education About Organizational Values and Culture	56%
Informing Employees of Organizational Performance Issues	38%
Providing Information and Feedback to Motivate and Improve Job Performance	31%

It's not surprising that 71 percent of respondents to a Watson Wyatt survey agreed that it is essential to link communications objectives to business strategy. Yet, how such an initiative is carried out can vary considerably from one organization to another. In years past, the human resources department was the preferred method for disseminating news and information. However, in recent years, the emphasis has begun to shift to the corporate communications department, reflecting the need to provide consistent, high-quality messages across departmental boundaries. Communication typically occurs through a combination of the following methods:

◆ Electronic mail,

◆ Newsletters,

◆ Live broadcasts or video,

◆ Intranets, and

◆ Group meetings.

Although human resources or corporate communications might create the message, successful organizations understand that managers must interpret, explain, and reinforce the organization's underlying communications strategy. If managers do not buy into the message and thoroughly understand it, they cannot create an unobstructed downstream flow. Furthermore, if they do not know or are not willing to handle questions, problems, and various other challenges, they cannot create an open channel for upstream communication. The same Watson Wyatt survey found that high-performance organizations achieve 50 percent better upstream communication than average organizations.

Figure 8.6
Emphasis in Communication Programs

Very strong or strong emphasis on	High-Performing Organizations	All Other Organizations
Helping Employees Understand the Business	77%	64%
Educating Employees About the Organization's Values and Culture	65%	54%
Informing Employees About the Organization's Progress Toward Business Objectives	65%	59%
Providing Feedback to Employees to Motivate and Help Them Improve Job Performance	33%	30%

Communication is made up of two parts: (1) facts, and (2) conclusions drawn from facts. How employees interpret information is just as important as the information itself. Moreover, it is crucial to provide people with information they can act on.

In order to succeed, a communications campaign must contain key elements that reach each stakeholder in a variety of ways. When well designed, the program will communicate relentlessly. In other words, no concerned individual will miss the messages because they will come in various forms and in frequent intervals.

The most effective communication is part of an overall strategic plan. It should be:

Intentional: Management should explicitly design the program to communicate values as well as information about different aspects of company life.

Differentiated: The plan should communicate what differentiates the organization in the marketplace and what gives it a competitive advantage.

Consistent: The message must be consistent. Rewards must reinforce the goals and objectives. For example, a company that deems itself a "high-performance organization" puts rewards in place for contribution, not longevity.

Valuable: The information must be valuable in the eyes of the receiver. It must have significant meaning for employees.

Research likewise indicates that financial success correlates with environments where:[11]

- ◆ Employees have easy access to technologies for communicating,

- ◆ Employees have the opportunity to give direct feedback to senior managers,

- ◆ Financial information and business plans and goals are shared with employees, and

- ◆ Employees have input into how the work gets done.

HR should encourage open communications about HR programs and policies. It should constantly tinker with its own programs and appraise their effectiveness based on selected data and employee feedback. Sometimes objective measures such as absenteeism or overuse of a particular program will send a clear signal that the program is not working. We have found that it never hurts to ask employees what they think, and it often helps a great deal. Employee surveys and focus groups can help, if the employer is willing to respond to valid issues and suggestions. This is especially true regarding the performance management and reward process. Staying aligned is the name of the game. If how HR manages performance and pay is not doing the job from the employee's view, it's an important message to hear.

Over the years we've noticed that successful business environments are characterized by the presence of some or all of the following:

1 Senior management recognizes the importance of communications in achieving business objectives and creates a climate conducive to information sharing.

2 Executive behavior is consistent with organizational communications.

3 Communications regarding corporate strategies that need employee engagement to succeed are based on a well-thought-out communications strategy.

4 Communication programs place a strong emphasis on helping employees understand their business.

5 The organization periodically shares information with employees about how the firm is doing in meeting its goals.

6 Individuals are expected to share business information with other employees through both formal and informal means.

7 Employee feedback on business issues is encouraged through formal communication channels.

8 Employees should be rewarded for effective communication.

Building the HR Brand

As we've discussed, being a great place to work ultimately pays dividends to the bottom line. *Fortune* magazine reports that the total annualized stock market return for the 49 of the "100 Best" companies that have been publicly traded has easily beaten the 3-year, 5-year and 10-year returns of the S&P 500.[12] Having a reputation for being a great place to work provides a competitive edge in today's talent-starved labor market that can't easily be matched by competitors.

What does it take to be listed as one of the best companies to work for? Having a basic idea of how to treat employees is a good place to start. The CEO of Hewlett Packard, Carly Fiorina, understood this when she said that the new streamlined company would retain the culture of respect and integrity that bears the brand the "HP Way." Such a statement characterizes a company's HR policies and programs in a way that is unique and differentiating.

Similarly, building an atmosphere of collegiality—of working collectively for the overall good of the company—builds employee commitment and engagement. Too often we have seen senior management, when faced with a critical human resource decision, ask "what's in it for me?" rather than "what's in it for the company?" Behavior begets behavior. If the leaders of the company don't see the greater good, neither will the rank and file. Special perquisites for senior executives similarly convey a we/they attitude. It's not surprising that companies that don't vary perquisites by position also seem to do better financially.[13]

Reported cultural attitudes such as encouraging teamwork and cooperation, being on a first name basis with top management, and more egalitarian titles that don't designate authority are also linked to better financial performance.[14] Twenty-six of *Fortune's* 100 best companies call their workers something other than "employees." Names like "associates," "team members," "co-workers," or "job owners" reinforce the "we're in this together" attitude and contribute to the quality of being a special place to work as an employee.[15]

Unique or special programs that underscore the company's commitment to meeting the needs of its employees also put a stamp on its people policies. In the early 1980s when *Fortune* first developed its "100 Best Companies to Work for in America" list, only two companies offered flextime to workers. Today, almost all report having flexible arrangements such as reduced summer hours, flexible schedules, job sharing, telecommuting, and compressed workweeks. Other companies report special programs like sabbaticals, wedding day limos, and vacation awards as part of their repertoire.[16]

But simply talking about fairness, integrity, or other positive attitudes or a new nomenclature for employees or special programs will not transform a mediocre employer into an employer of choice. A friend recently recounted a story that illustrates this point. As a young man he worked for the subsidiary of a large company. The subsidiary was not doing very well and there was a great amount of disaffection among its employees. The subsidiary management did employee-attitude surveys and installed a 360-degree feedback program—all in an attempt to demonstrate that management cared about its employees. Nothing helped. He was later transferred to a second subsidiary with the same parent company which was doing well. The subsidiary eschewed special HR programs. In fact, there was no need to ask employees how they felt about certain things because the managers knew. Human resource policy ensured that everyone was treated as an equal, communication was direct and open, and behavior from top to bottom was aligned with the subsidiary strategy. My friend's comments to me were that HR "band-aids" don't work, its got to be the "real deal."

The "real deal" in this case means an organization that has thought about itself and decided that it wants to create a unique "brand" on how it treats its employees. As Figure 8.7 suggests, a would-be employer of choice moves away from random policies, or simply copying generic approaches offered by competitors, best practices, or (God forbid) consultants. Instead, it asks

◆ What is it about how we treat people that would make them want to work here?

◆ What is there about what we do that would excite employee interest and commitment?

◆ What do we do that demonstrates our commitment to employee welfare and helps employees negotiate the day-to-day compromises surrounding employment?

Figure 8.7
The Branded Experience

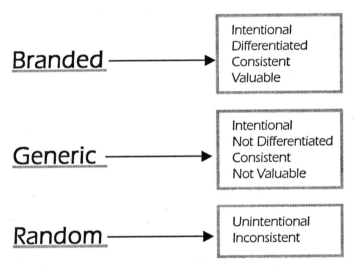

Conclusion

A company starts building its people brand when it decides what is unique about the way it treats its people or the way it wants to treat its people and tells its employees about it. It takes its next step when it adopts programs and consistent behaviors that support its people policies. It completes the circle when everyone in the company—from top to bottom—can state why it is a special place to be. That's when an organization knows it has an HR brand.

Notes

1 Global Oil is a fictional name.

2 Bank of the World is a fictional name.

3 Ronald B. Morgan, Jack E. Smith, "Staffing the New Workplace: Selecting and Promoting for Quality Improvement" (Milwaukee: ASQ Quality Press, March 1996), p. 202.

4 Ronald B. Morgan, Jack E. Smith.

5 "The Human Capital Index: Linking Human Capital and Shareholder Value," Watson Wyatt Worldwide study, 2000.

6 "Employees Speak Out: New Study Links Employee Satisfaction to Job Training," *Business Wire*, September 7, 1998.

7 "Strategic Rewards: The New Employment Deals," Watson Wyatt Worldwide Survey Report, 1999/2000.

8 Jeffrey Pfeffer, *Competitive Advantage Through People: Unleashing the Power of the Work Force* (Boston: Harvard Business School Press, 1994), pp. 45-46.

9 Ibid.

10 "1999 Communications Study: Linking Communications With Strategy to Achieve Business Goals," Watson Wyatt Worldwide study, 1999.

11 "The Human Capital Index" study.

12 "The 100 Best Companies to Work For," *Fortune*, January 10, 2000, p. 90.

13 "The Human Capital Index" study.

14 Ibid.

15 *Fortune*, p. 96.

16 *Fortune*, pp. 90-92.

Index